Finding a Guy like Gilbert – a Dating Manifesto

Finding a Guy like Gilbert – a Dating Manifesto

by Penelope Winters

ILLUSTRATED BY
PENELOPE WINTERS

"Penelope Winters takes you on such a heartfelt journey through the challenges of finding your happily ever after. You feel as though she is accompanying you every step of the way. Penelope's valuable tools and warm, open-hearted support make this a must-read for anyone looking for love!"

Debra Newell. *Debra's incredible survival story, told in the breakout Bravo series "Dirty John" is known worldwide. She is a tireless advocate and helper to women trapped in abusive and coercive control relationships.*

"'Finding a Guy Like Gilbert – a Dating Manifesto' is a delightful little book that I found completely relatable. Definitely an eye-opener. As I go through my own book of revelations I find myself thinking of this book! A beautiful, short read."

Sommer Wayne Dyer, *daughter of Dr Wayne Dyer, avid reader, eternal optimist, horse person, thinker, artist, and student.*

"There is so much sense in this book. I love Penelope's no-nonsense honesty combined with warmth and wisdom. A very helpful book."

Marianne Power, *author of "Help Me", writer and freelance journalist.*

"This book is full of wisdom and wonderful insights not just into love and dating but into how to live the kind of life you want to live. Written with heart and soul and compassion I recommend it to anyone who happens to be human."

Victoria Mary Clarke, *journalist, author and designer.*

"In a world that can seem so full of cynicism, I found Penelope's unabashed celebration of romance a complete delight. And when the first task is to read my beloved childhood book 'Anne of Green Gables', well, this is self-help with soul. I love that Penelope reminds us that kindness is king, and that any man that can be a little more Gilbert Blythe is worthy of our love. A sensitive, humorous and generous read, I really enjoyed dipping in and out of this unique book as a reminder of the magic of love—and it starting with ourselves."

Irene O'Brien, *TV stylist, presenter, and writer.*

"Never have I read a book that felt more like my own personal journal. The stories of past woes that Penelope shared resonated so much with me. Surprisingly, as a result, a cynic like me, has gained hope for the future. A beautiful mix of advice and an honest account of personal experiences, humorously written."

Sinéad Ní Uallacháin, *RTE broadcaster; and one third of the podcast Beo ar Éigean.*

"Truly hilarious—can't get enough of this!"

Caroline Grace-Cassidy, author and screenwriter.

"Belly laugh inducing book, that touches on all emotions. There is a lesson in this book for all of us. Raw, real and a must read!"

Caitlín Nic Aoidh, TG4 weather presenter.

"My mother always told me if you don't love yourself, no one else will. That message is at the heart of 'Finding a Guy Like Gilbert – a Dating Manifesto'. In this part memoir / part self help guide Penelope Winters generously brings the reader into her own personal life, documenting the ups and the downs, to give context to her journey to love. You can tell the author's main aim is for others to find the happy ending she did."

Susan Keogh, broadcast journalist who presents Newstalk Breakfast on Saturday and Sunday mornings.

"This beautifully written book will help you to unblock your 'trapped emotions', as Penelope describes them. She shares her personal experiences with honesty and humour encouraging you to take heart, a healthy heart, as you search for love, including love of self. Her affirmations are stepping stones to feeling anything is possible."

Maura O Neill, Agony Aunt for the Sunday World and author of 'Our Place', a collection of poetry.

"A must-read guidebook for the modern woman-practical, funny and a huge comfort."

Susan Webster, Family Law Solicitor.

"'Finding a Guy Like Gilbert – a Dating Manifesto' is a fabulous, fun read full of honest tips and answers about dating, from where we've gone wrong in the past to managing our expectations. If we love ourselves we won't have to settle for second best."

Tina Koumarianos was Social Editor and Agony Aunt at IMAGE Magazine for many years before joining Virgin Media One's Elaine Show as their resident Agony Aunt each week.

A Catalogue record for this book is available from the British Library

Book layout by Karl Hunt
Edited by May Lan Tan
Cover design by Rob Allen

ISBN 9798612721864

Contents

CONTENTS

CONTENTS

"For Billy and my wonderful primary school teacher,
Frances O Connor."

Foreword by Julie Jay

Julie Jay is a comedian and podcaster. Having supported a number of comedy stars, including Tommy Tiernan, Ardal O'Hanlon and Des Bishop, she is now determined to be the headline act in her own life.

I only recently got around to watching Sex and the City, in which the inequity of dating in New York City causes even the buoyant Charlotte York to exclaim, 'I have been dating since I was fifteen. I'm exhausted. Where *is* he?'

While I immediately empathised with her frustration, no thirty-something woman in Ireland has been dating since age fifteen, bar the minority of girls who had access to tanning salons and to their elder sisters' Babyliss hair straighteners. Rather, we shifted a guy for a decade or two before finding out they weren't looking for anything serious. On more than one occasion, this invariably led to us sobbing into our garlic cheese chips before swearing to venture beyond the peninsula in the hope of finding an urbanite who wouldn't view eye contact as something one did only once, surrounded by friends and family, in a church.

The blueprint for most of my adult relationships was provided by *Pretty Woman,* with its plethora of important life lessons: embrace your ginger curl, always floss, and never kiss on the mouth. This film is largely to blame for my exceptionally late understanding of contraception—many's a time I whipped out a gold coin in a bid to avoid unwanted pregnancy—and my penchant for emotionally unavailable men. *(He's successful, yet sad because he doesn't build anything! This really puts my life on the streets to shame!)* It also led me to believe that someday I would meet a man who would defy his fear of heights to whisk me off to a life of being a corporate widow. Oh, how I dared to dream!

I have come to realise that if a relationship does not work out, rather than being the fault of the individuals concerned, it is simply that the dynamic itself does not work. When you stop playing the blame game, it is truly liberating. During many of my break-ups, I ran my life by committee, ringing friend upon friend until I hit upon that one poor ally who endorsed what I had already determined to be my next course of action: a long text, a letter of apology, a life drawing. To step back and say, *I am worth more than this*, you really are leaving a space in your life for some true emotional alchemy to happen.

Not so long ago, I met a thoroughly lovely young man who is definitely first husband material. Reader, I moved in with him. Having not enjoyed this kind of love for a long time and having convinced myself I would never find it again, I had built a happy life centred not on another person's happiness but on my own, and so I'm more resilient than ever. Should things not pan out as I hope they will—natural death taking one of us in our winter years, when we are basking in the joy of *Homes Under the Hammer* and weekly colonoscopies—I know I'll be okay. And that, for me, is a triumph of cognitive evolution.

That discovery is very much in line with the ambitions of this book. As Carrie says at the end of the series finale:

"The most exciting, challenging and significant relationship of all is the one you have with yourself. And if you find someone to love the you *you* love, well, that's just fabulous."

I hope you'll read this, enjoy it, and find comfort in our shared experience.

Julie Jay
Comedian

Foreword by Lydia Davis

A few years after founding dinner dating company Table8 in 2012, Lydia Davis moved into matchmaking and has worked at a top London agency. She was selected as a Dating Expert of the Year finalist at the UK Dating Awards in 2017 and has been featured and quoted in press worldwide. Her current venture is Toffee, a niche dating app.

Having spent many years helping single women, including myself, to find love, I know first-hand how disheartening it can sometimes be. This book is for women of all ages who have felt this way and who may believe that they're just not going to be lucky in love. In her warm and accessible style, Penelope Winters shares with us the story of how she went from hopeless and hapless to happily married within a short timeframe, and how you can do the same. This wonderfully uplifting book provides you with the right tools and attitude to help raise your hopes again and meet the man of your dreams. There's someone out there for everyone—you just need to believe it.

I feel it's important to reflect upon your dating journey and learn from it, to visualise and realise that there's someone who will love you for who you are, and finally to know that you deserve this and have so much to offer someone else. You'll find out how to get your confidence back, find your dating sass, and find real, true, exciting, intimate love. Penelope bravely shares with us her own story, which will be incredibly relatable for so many women all over the world.

Readers will really connect with this honest, inspiring and heart-warming tale of the author's journey to love. She includes practical suggestions, and some of them are somewhat quirky but they're fun. I hope you'll enjoy this book as much as I did. Get reading and invite the man of your dreams into your life!

Lydia Davis
Matchmaker

Preface

I always considered myself to be utterly hopeless in matters of the heart. At age thirty-three, plagued by severe OCD, I resigned myself to remaining single forever. Feeling utterly devoid of hope, I signed up for group therapy in the form of a Louise L. Hay *Heal Your Life* course. Thanks to the encouragement of the teacher and the other class members, I found myself believing for the first time that I might actually deserve love. This was the very first step of a life-changing journey, of therapy, meditation, affirmation and many other practices, which brought me to a place in my life where I began to expect the love, respect and devotion of a wonderful man. In life, you get no less than you expect, and so it is imperative that you start to anticipate the arrival of your ideal partner. Today I am happily married. Looking back on how my life had turned around within a relatively short span of time, I became inspired to write a memoir and self-help guide for others who, just like me, might need a friend to help them to navigate the world of dating and relationships. This book documents the path that ultimately led me to the man who has turned out to be right for me. It comes straight from my heart, and I hope it will find a home in yours.

— P.W.

WHEN YOU SPOT A COLLEAGUE IN THE SELF-HELP SECTION OF YOUR LOCAL BOOKSHOP AND YOU'RE NOT SURE IF SHE'S SEEN YOU SO YOU DROP THE BOOKS BUT CAN'T DECIDE WHAT TO DO NEXT

YOU ARE AT THE STARTING LINE!

DEFINITION

Gilbert = a nice guy who likes you back.

Invite Love into Your Life

You may have spent the last ten years avoiding unsolicited advice about dating, relationships and men, because the person offering it does not know you, what you want, what is right for you or what you deserve. If this is the case, you doubtless will have long been bending the ears of your friends and relatives with all the qualities you're not seeking in a man and all the ways in which the men you've met thus far have fallen short of your expectations. Don't feel disheartened; see this as an opportunity to grow. You can stop repeating past mistakes and start to learn from them and move forward simply by welcoming feedback and using it constructively to fine-tune your approach.

Many women expend too much energy analysing text messages from men who aren't interested in them, and too little time listening to those who have been successful in matters of the heart. If you are single and have a strong desire to change this, then you might wish to consider opening up to what may seem like the quirky, nonsensical suggestions of well-meaning friends. If these friends are happily partnered with suitable matches, they will have played the dating game with success. You might start to view them as role models. Do not dismiss their advice. Listen to them because they have accomplished much in a field where you have yet to excel. They may share valuable advice about how to turn things around, beat the odds, overcome low self-esteem, recover from previous heartbreak, and build a solid relationship.

You are poised at the starting line. You have bought this book, which indicates that you acknowledge that you have work to do on yourself. You realise that the men in your life are not the problem. The problem is that you have invited them into a place where they do not rightfully belong. They are not your match, nor are you theirs. You should also consider taking others' advice from time to time, instead of immediately dismissing it as not relevant to you or your situation. If you truly knew what was best for you, you wouldn't still be looking for love with all the wrong people.

Some people are lucky. They seem to instinctively know who is right and what will work for them. Wherever they go, they meet someone, embark upon a relationship, and find happiness with that person. Other people (and I count myself among them) have to expend so much energy before they can find love. We shine in our careers and enjoy close friendships that nurture our souls, but we find romance hard to come by. Even if you're not the type who falls easily into relationships, you can still find a wonderful and fulfilling one. You can start now, by cultivating an attitude of openness. This means letting go of your attachment to viewing your story as unique, unknowable and unsolvable.

I wrote this book for women like me, who, for whatever reason, have never easily found love. Some of the most beautiful and talented women in the world are less than lucky in love but we know that this is not a reflection of our attractiveness or our personality or anything else. More often, it is a reflection of how we feel about ourselves, and about men and relationships, at any given time.

I have known some women whom men found irresistible. These women were not necessarily the most beautiful women I've known, but they all shared a sense of their importance in this world and an expectation that men would find them attractive. Men love women who love themselves. It really is that simple. If you value yourself, the people around you are more likely to value you as well.

You may never be that woman with mass appeal, but why would you want to be? Aren't you looking for someone who's a bit more discerning? All you need is one man to find you appealing. There's a man out there seeking a woman exactly like you. If you can believe that there is one available man living in your proximity who will find you irresistible, you're already halfway there. Do you accept that, by the law of averages, there must be at least one person living within, say, a ten-kilometre radius who will find you incredibly attractive? (This is a conservative estimate. There are likely many more!) You've acknowledged that a potential partner is living nearby. You're just a few steps away from having an ardent admirer. How does it feel? This realisation alone should be enough to give your confidence a boost.

When I was in my early thirties, I had been single for what felt like forever. I was not attracted to the men who were interested in me. Although I was very discerning when composing lists of the qualities I'd wish for in my ideal man; in reality, I wasn't at all picky. Nor did I always act with integrity. My friends would set me up with men they knew, and on more than one occasion I ducked out at the earliest opportunity because I didn't like something about the guy: his shoes; his upper arms; his grammar. At times I even felt dispirited that my friends viewed these men as suitable matches. In behaving this way, I was being rude to the men in question and showing disrespect to the friends who had kindly arranged dates for me. I eventually came to realise that, in pursuing men with whom I had nothing in common, I was selling myself short and dishonouring my true nature. By being dismissive and critical of others, I was acting like some of the men I had met on dating sites whose behaviour I abhorred. Wayne Dyer talks of how we attract *what we are*, not what we want. How could I have attracted honesty, kindness and humility when I was not practising these values?

I'd like to share with you the steps I took and the philosophy I embraced during my quest to find a true and lasting love. While these are merely suggestions, I hope you'll try out some or all of them, and have fun doing so. Please don't dismiss any of these without at least entertaining the thought of giving them a whirl. Each of us has individual tastes and values, so you'll need to adapt these suggestions and exercises to suit your own personality and lifestyle.

When I embarked upon this journey, I had zero belief in my ability to find love. In my attempt to remain hopeful, I took a multipronged approach. I tried many things that felt right, and some things that didn't feel as comfortable, and I can honestly say I enjoyed every minute of it. I hope that you'll enjoy your journey too.

I want you to consider me as one of those friends whose advice you have sought (and perhaps dismissed) over the years. I'm a friend you can trust. I'm here to help you to prepare yourself for love and open yourself up to the possibility of having a wonderful relationship. I will help you more than the friend who is forever promising to set you up with her boyfriend's brother-in-law, best friend or cousin but never makes good on her promise. I have your best interests at heart. I have been where you are, and I will bring you exactly where you need to be to attract your soul mate.

I believe completely in your ability to manifest love. I'm proud of you for having shown up for this. Take these steps to invite love into your life. When it comes, you will be ready.

STEP 1: Clear out the emotional clutter

I spent the entirety of my twenties locked in the painful cycle of food addiction. While I believed that eating was the only truly pleasurable aspect of living, I was terrified of gaining weight. I had committed to maintaining a non-fluctuating weight of 112 pounds, and this ruled my life. I lived in a state of perpetual stress. I deprived myself of food that I wanted. I never ate out, because I would be sure to consume my daily allowance of calories even before the dessert arrived. I never went on holiday, fearing the temptation to overeat. I found little enjoyment in anything except food, which had to be rationed, regretted, thrown up or burnt off. I wished I were one of those people with an impossibly high metabolism, who seemed to be able to eat as much as they want of whatever they like without ever gaining weight. Compulsive overeating provided distraction from my loneliness and pain. After bingeing on food, I would be overcome with self-loathing and try to work off the excess calories in the gym the following morning. The gym could not open early enough for me.

I was lonely and felt that my life was not worth living. I received no pleasure out of life. I was living with an addiction that was destroying my life. To add insult to injury, it didn't even have the life-threatening status of bulimia or anorexia. I felt that many people thought that binge-eating disorder was merely another word for greed. Often, I ate to the point of feeling violently ill. I wasn't proficient in throwing up—it could take me hours to achieve and did not create the same high that I got from exercising. Every minute not spent working in the job that I disliked, I would spend exercising in a gym full of people that I didn't know. One Sunday morning, I looked at myself in the mirror at the gym and said to myself: *Enough.*

I decided to find my way back to a normal and healthy relationship with food. And, despite the fact that a therapist had once told me I would probably never achieve this, I did. I knew I owed that much to myself. From that moment and as a result of the decision to try, my life took off in a new direction. I was now heading towards a place where love was possible.

Recovery is a gradual process. Many of the small steps I made were centred on attempting to recover my childhood self, who saw the potential for laughter and pleasure everywhere. I returned to activities I had enjoyed as a child, such as drawing and writing. I felt as if I were feasting on words and pictures instead of on food. I started to heal. Eventually I succeeded in setting myself free from this destructive obsession. I returned to the self I had been as a teenager, who was slim but never thought about diets or deprivation and found the whole topic terribly prosaic. These days, I like food, but I don't live for it. My greatest pleasures are reading, writing, watching TV crime dramas with my husband, spending time with my baby son, talking and laughing with friends, and doing the cryptic crossword.

Many women struggle with some form of eating disorder, and it cuts both ways as our bodies are enmeshed with how we perceive ourselves and how society perceives us. The roots of eating disorders are planted during childhood and are so deeply embedded that we often don't know why we eat the way we do. During my twenties, I would cut short a perfectly pleasant date simply because I was worrying about how many calories I'd consume over the course of the meal. I returned home early from a holiday abroad because I couldn't tolerate lounging around in the sun, reading and eating, and enjoying myself. I wasted so much of my life. I sometimes wonder whether my husband and I would have even made it past the second date if I hadn't already been on the path to recovery when we met.

It's advisable to undertake recovery under the guidance of a professional. Find a therapist with whom you feel comfortable. Your therapist should support and challenge you, and it's helpful if they understand that recovery should be focused upon reward rather than punishment. Ideally this person should be on the same page as you. When one therapist advised me to eat popcorn before going to bed so that I wouldn't wake up hungry during the night, I instinctively knew that this was not the right person to help me overcome my preoccupation with food.

In therapy, you will address the unresolved issues and trapped emotions that are holding you back from finding love. At a point in my life when I was consumed with anger, a warm and wise therapist provided a useful analogy. She urged me to visualise myself sitting in a carriage and holding the reins of a horse. I had been travelling down a road of anger, and this horse could only take me further along this same road, which led to misery. I had resisted letting go of my anger because I felt entitled to it. She explained to me that the only way to travel along a different path—one that led to joy—was to let go of the reins, climb down from the carriage that could travel only on this particular, well-worn track, and to climb into another carriage that would take me down an entirely different route. As I pictured myself releasing the reins, I finally let go of the anger, hatred and pain that had come to consume me. While connecting with your anger can be healthy and mobilising, holding onto it for too long can destroy you, as it nearly destroyed me.

Sadness, anger and fear are all part of the process of recovery. Allow yourself to connect with these emotions, but do not hold onto them and remember to ration your self-pity. You may treat yourself to a dose of self-pity on your own time, but don't subject others to it. This would be like inviting them over to your house on a Saturday night to watch you binge on cheesecake—what's in it for them? While you can talk through your feelings with empathetic, interested friends who care deeply for you, please resist the impulse to divulge all of your dating dilemmas to your co-workers or random acquaintances at the gym. Don't dominate the conversation; there has to be some give and take. It's fine to talk things out, and to seek useful, practical and loving advice from friends and family members, but just don't make it all about you.

In order to make enough room in your life for love, you must first clear out the clutter. This means dealing with addiction or anything else that is holding you back, including toxic emotions that threaten to pollute the relationships that you hope to form. Addiction is a major roadblock on the path to love, as it prevents you from having a full and healthy relationship with anyone else. Your preferred substance or behaviour takes precedence over everyone and everything else, including yourself. Emotional baggage also falls under the category of addiction, as it is an addiction to the past and to unhealthy patterns. It is a long journey back to joyful living, but it's one that you have to make if you are serious in your intent to be happy and find love.

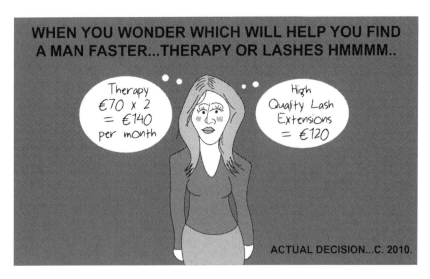

INVEST IN THERAPY, MEN WON'T NOTICE THE LASHES!

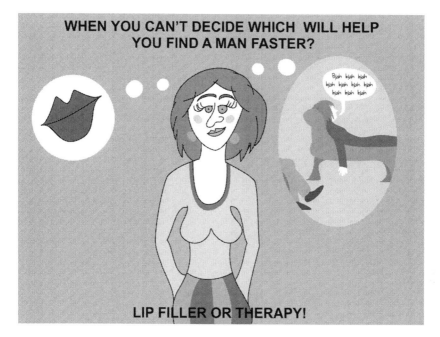

AGAIN, INVEST IN THERAPY, MEN WON'T NOTICE THE LIPS!

STEP 2: Change your type to Gilbert Blythe
(otherwise known as Nice Guy Who Likes You Back)

This step is non-negotiable. Although you may believe you are attracted to a specific type of person, and that this attraction is fixed and unalterable; there are many different types of men that you must learn to overlook or erase from your line of vision (just as there are various kinds of unsuitable women whom men should avoid). Looking back over my life, I see a pattern of attraction to men who were emotionally unavailable. I have many friends who have consistently selected men who are selfish, self-destructive, unfaithful or lazy—the list goes on.

When we strip it all down, the only life partner you should consider is one who shares your core values and goals, who loves and respects you, and whose eyes light up when you walk into the room. Of course, you will have other specifications. Some women seek someone who's cultured, while others would happily forgo this in favour of a good laugh. An unavailable man may intrigue you more than an overly eager one, and nothing will pique your interest more than someone who seems to be indifferent to your presence. You may do everything in your power to attract his attention, and still he doesn't respond. Even the coldest and most detached of men will lose their minds in pursuit of a woman who captures their heart, so, if he doesn't seem interested, he probably isn't. Instead of taking his disinterest and indifference as an invitation to obsess, you need to look around and see who is paying attention to you.

For every idiot who will mess you around if given the opportunity, there is a fantastic person who will love, respect and support you. It's so easy to become disheartened—that taxi journey home alone on a Saturday night serves only to reinforce the fear that no one will ever be interested in you. You wonder if you're actually invisible. You're not a superstitious person, but you have begun to wonder if some people are cursed when it comes to relationships. Will you ever find a loving partner?

Don't allow yourself to become overwhelmed or despondent. If you take it personally, this will only slow you down. You've been trying to force a puzzle piece into a place it doesn't belong. You just need to step back and take another look to see where it might fit.

You can look to literature and film for examples of loyal, devoted men who will go to any lengths to win the heart of their beloved. I became acquainted with the notion of the nice guy when I read Lucy Maud Montgomery's *Anne of Green Gables* series. Reading of how the young Gilbert Blythe relentlessly pursued Anne, long before I learned to see myself as unlovable, I presumed that this would someday happen to me. I was just as attractive, smart, fun and ambitious as Anne.

Later, when I experienced rejection, as everyone does at some point, I didn't integrate that rejection naturally into my being and grow from it, learn more about myself, and toughen up; I took it as a decree sent from above—a confirmation of my inadequacy. I have always been a sensitive soul, a hopeless romantic who tried to hide behind a cynical veneer, rejecting people before they could reject me.

During my awkward adolescent years, I was never one of the popular girls. I had red hair, pale skin, and small breasts, traits denigrated by my peers at that time, though I've since come to understand that they are beautiful. I internalised my shame about being different and directed my anger and frustration towards myself. At a house party, I was the only girl in my year group who was not asked to dance by any of the boys. I remember standing there alone, feeling as if everyone was looking at me with pity. At twenty-one, I spent a year studying in France without ever being approached by a man, while my friends—many of whom had boyfriends back home—were batting away offers from men. These experiences reinforced my image of myself as unattractive. It became a self-fulfilling prophecy. I entered social situations with my head bowed. Fearing ridicule, I didn't initiate conversations with men. In my early thirties, I finally realised that if I wanted to be the kind of woman I admire, I would have to be more confident. I knew I needed to do a lot of work on myself, and to start filtering out the kind of men who had not proven to be a good match for me.

Anne of Green Gables and its five sequels are all beautifully written and never fail to lift my spirits. If life imitates art, any premise conceived in literature can become a reality. Over the years, whenever

I have felt miserable and hopeless, I have found comfort in this. It assured me that there were many Gilbert Blythes out there—one for every Anne.

The moment Gilbert sets eyes on Anne, he completely falls for her. He adores and admires her, seeks out her company, and relentlessly pursues her. He is kind, clever, funny, handsome and loyal. While Anne is not the prettiest girl in Avonlea Gilbert discerns in her a beauty that cannot be outshined. He sees her failings, and gently challenges her to relinquish her silly, proud ways and overly romantic ideals.

Many years before meeting my husband, I told a friend I would like to marry a man whom others saw as being incredibly kind. Recently, my brother described my husband as one of the nicest people he had ever met. He then promptly revised his description to *the nicest person*. My wish came true, but it didn't happen overnight. In my early thirties I began a process of transformation. This journey of discovery brought me to a place I had never been before. I began to actually like myself and to respect myself enough to want better. I've ended up marrying this great guy, but I've had to do a lot of work on myself. Fortunately, this type of work is quite enjoyable.

It's time to stop paying attention to the type of men you don't want in your life and to keep your mind and heart set on the Gilberts of this world. Be mindful of what you think and say. Ease up on the self-deprecation. Your subconscious hears everything you say. Instead of talking about your turnoffs and deal-breakers, talk about what you'd most like to achieve in a relationship. Life has a funny way of giving us the things on which we focus our attention.

If you and your friends are sitting around and analysing a man's mysterious and sudden withdrawal of affection, you must give up that ghost right away. If he appears to blow hot and cold, this is never going to develop into a relationship. Even if it does, over time you will grow to resent the way he treats you. Don't settle for a man who fails to appreciate your beauty and worth.

Men who run for the hills whenever a woman appears to reciprocate their affection are emotionally unavailable. Because they don't value themselves highly, they believe you must be a little crazy if you like them. Don't be one of these people, and don't be with one of them. If you choose to pursue a cold, forbidding man who keeps you at arm's length, you will spend your whole life trying to claw your way back into his affections after each rejection. Each time he seems to tire of you, you will have to feign disinterest and apathy in order to regain his attention and reignite his passions. He does not like you for who you are; he likes you when you appear not to like him. You deserve much better than this. Such a man has many issues to unravel and emotional knots to untie. Let him do that on his own time. On the other hand, a man who's interested in you and unafraid to show it has both good sense and excellent taste.

Men who withhold praise and affection will erode your self-worth. We all need to hear that we are valued and appreciated. Paying compliments is an indication of generosity. Men who ration compliments will be just as stingy with their time and money.

Men who criticise you in subtle and insidious ways will punish you for as long as you're with them. I knew a man who guessed the age of every woman he met at one year older than he knew her to be, having made enquiries beforehand. He hoped that making women feel insecure about their appearance would give him the upper hand. More often than not, this worked. Men who put you down to make you feel insecure and vulnerable are insecure and vulnerable themselves. Anyone who plays power games or competes with you does not have your best interests at heart. Partners should support, praise and encourage each other.

Men who have addiction issues have no room in their lives for anyone else. You cannot rescue them, and you may destroy yourself in the process of trying.

If you are drawn to cold, distant, flighty, cruel, damaged or emotionally complicated men, you need to start to recognise them as the troubled individuals that they are. If you want to be happy in the long term, you must change your type. Recondition yourself to feel attracted to nice, courteous, friendly men.

Your first task is to read *Anne of Green Gables*. I would also recommend reading the other books in the series. *Anne of the Island* has long been my favourite because it focuses on the growing relationship between Anne and Gilbert. Watch the film adaptation of *Anne of Green Gables*, produced, written and directed by Kevin Sullivan, starring Megan Follows and Jonathan Crombie. As much as I adored the books, I preferred the films. When you see how Gilbert adores Anne and makes unthinkable sacrifices for her, you will never want to look at another unavailable bad boy.

Imagine how it would feel to have someone look at you the way Gilbert looks at Anne. Picture how glorious it would be to bask in such admiration and respect. Daydream a little. Imagine waking up every morning knowing you are with an amazing man who's flattered and proud that you reciprocate his feelings and wants to stay with you.

Now is the time to reconfigure the template of your ideal man, because there's nothing fun, exciting or romantic about dating a man who will always be looking over your shoulder for his next conquest. Read the books, watch the films, and start to dream.

Will them into reality. On your next date, ask yourself: *Is this how Gilbert would have treated Anne?*

STEP 3: Write, recite and sing affirmations for attracting love

I really enjoyed this part of the process, and I think you will too. You may feel powerless as you wait for a man to become sufficiently interested in you, and to muster the courage to approach you. You may not want to go around asking men out, and this is perfectly understandable. You may be asking yourself whether there is anything you can do to expedite the arrival of a wonderful man into your life. Yes, there certainly is, and you can do it right in the comfort of your own armchair. *Believe it and you'll see it.* You may have heard some variation of this axiom before. How do you go about achieving that? How do you acquire the belief that you were put on this earth to be half of a wonderfully loving partnership, if you feel with every fibre of your being that you are unworthy of being loved?

By the time I was in my early thirties, I had come to despair of meeting that special someone. I had fallen into a pattern of dating men I didn't really find attractive, in hopes that, due to their own lack of physical charm, they would appreciate me all the more. This strategy never panned out. In fact, the men who should have considered themselves most fortunate to have me in the first place were the ones who treated me the worst. They seemed to think that they could do better than me. There is a limit to how many times you can ignore a man's roving eye, shoddy excuses or ungracious manners.

Here is something you can do to speed up the process. Affirming your strengths and other positive aspects empowers you. In this way, you can reprogram yourself to expect to be truly valued. In the past, you were at the mercy of your parents' programming.

While some of this may have been healthy, other parts may have been damaging. Today, you can seize the opportunity to start to change the way you think, thereby changing the way you feel about yourself and your life, luck, fate and relationships. While it's true that a course of written affirmations will not immediately cause you to emerge fully confident and assured of your worthiness at all times and in all situations, you just might raise your spirits a little, and that can be enough to attract someone wonderful into your life.

When you get to truly know and love someone, neither one of you will be turned off by the other's vulnerability; you will be fully understanding and supportive of each other. When we drop all our pretences and show our true selves in the presence of someone we love, we are exposed and vulnerable. In that honesty and openness lies the enhanced potential for a true heart connection. If one of us is trying to be someone or something that we're not, there can be no authentic connection between us.

By setting an affirmation, you are guiding yourself towards the knowledge that you deserve to find love, to be lucky in love just long enough to draw a wonderful man a little closer to you. And I believe that this can be achieved within a matter of a few minutes each day. By elevating your vibration for even a short period every day, you start to radiate positive expectancy, enabling you to draw your ideal man closer. Nobody is bursting with confidence 24/7. Everyone's journey is punctuated by peaks and troughs. Even if you only spend a few minutes each day truly believing that love is yours and that it will materialise in time, you start to draw him, and that loving experience, a little closer.

I had so much fun composing my affirmations. I particularly love ones that rhyme because they are easy to remember and a joy to write out and recite. I would encourage you to compose your own affirmations using language that reflects you, your aspirations and your personality, and makes you feel excited and hopeful. Below you will find a few affirmations that I composed for myself, as well as for friends who were looking to attract love into their lives.

In many cases, the greatest barrier to finding someone truly special is an unhealthy attachment to a relationship that is leading nowhere. Simply removing this barrier can allow you to clearly see the opportunities for love and growth that have been right in front of you all along. It is incredibly hard to let go, and it can be hardest to let go of the people who have had the least positive impact on our lives. I wrote the following affirmation while I was struggling to move on from an unfulfilling situation that I was clinging to, even though it had long ceased to bring me any joy.

I let go and I trust in a Higher Plan,

I let go and make way for my ideal man,

I let go, letting go is a gift for me,

I let go, it feels great to be finally free.

Before I met my husband, I was seeing a man I had known for a long time. Our mutual friends had all told me that he was not a keeper. Because he worked in London for part of the week and held a fast-paced job, I expected very little contact from him. My low expectations served as a form of self-protection. Because I knew I was never going to get the level of interest from him that I wanted and needed, I told myself it would be unrealistic to expect more than a few text messages during the week. While I knew that this was not a proper relationship, I hung on desperately, waiting for him to realise what a catch I was. It was hard to let go. If I had been stronger, and if I had felt better about myself, I would have ended the relationship much earlier than I actually did. I want you to learn from my mistakes. It is often more difficult to disentangle oneself from a deeply unsatisfactory relationship than it is to leave a mediocre one. By acknowledging that you feel unfulfilled and disrespected, you are also admitting that you have wasted months, years or even decades of your life. But it is never too late to treat yourself with respect, to listen to your heart and to find joy.

Always affirm your desired state in the present tense—as if it has already materialised. Believe that you are attracting your ideal partner into your life. With each repetition you are drawing him closer, summoning the life and love that are rightfully yours into existence. Maybe you're sceptical; maybe you're optimistic. When someone has full confidence that whatever force they believe in—whether that's providence, the universe or the gods—has their best interests at heart and is on their side, pulling strings for them behind the scenes, they feel more relaxed, thereby becoming infinitely more attractive. On the other hand, a person who believes that most outcomes are beyond their control tends to act and appear stressed and controlling. Instead of struggling to grasp that bar of soap in the bath, you would be better off relaxing. That elusive soap bar will eventually make its way into your grip, naturally and easily. Yes, it is hard to let go, and to have faith that things will work themselves out. But what you have been doing thus far has not yielded your desired result, right? So why not give this step a go?

I composed this affirmation especially for those who don't feel fully deserving of a loving relationship with a fabulous man at this moment in time:

> *I deserve to have an amazing man*
>
> *who thinks that I'm amazing too,*
>
> *a man who loves me with all his heart,*
>
> *and for whom my love is deep and true.*

None of us is fully confident in every area of life. We each have vulnerabilities and weak points. All of us have been damaged in some way by people who didn't know better or couldn't do better. Hemingway said it beautifully when he wrote that the world breaks every man but that some of us are strong at the broken places. Your greatest weaknesses may provide your most valuable life lessons and opportunities for growth.

Some of us may believe that we are not intelligent enough; others may feel unattractive. There is an endless list of potential hang-ups and perceived inadequacies. But even the apparently gloriously happy person sitting opposite you in your meditation class has her own struggles and crosses to bear. Most of us know where our own broken places lie. Try to write positive affirmations regarding the issues that cause you the most pain. Locate the power within yourself as you write, say, chant or sing your affirmations, and aim to repeat them as often as you possibly can throughout your day. If you are feeling creative, why not try making your own affirmation cards? This process is fun, enjoyable and light-hearted. Affirmations may not be everyone's cup of tea at first, but many people have found a lot of power in them. Be light and playful when creating them, selecting language that truly reflects you and gets you excited and hopeful about the future. Generating that sort of positivity and experiencing that intense expectation, even for only a few minutes a day, will be enough to compel the type of romance that you desire.

Shortly after finishing school, I read the classic *Feel the Fear and Do It Anyway* by the wonderful and inspiring Susan Jeffers. That's how I became acquainted with the potential of affirmations to change people's lives. I put them into practice for a while, when my confidence was at an all-time low and I was feeling unattractive and overweight. They worked, but only for as long as I practised them. I resisted fully committing to a lifetime of daily affirmation, for the same reason I had held off for a long time on joining a gym. If I started to look and feel really good, I might have to keep it up for the rest of my life—at least, for as long as my mental and physical health mattered to me. This option continued floating about in my consciousness, but I didn't seriously consider it until, at age thirty-three, I experienced a bout of serious anxiety for the second time in my life. I was forced to take a step back and reassess what I was doing. Mainly, I was wasting opportunities by avoiding challenges, due to my fear of failure, of negative exposure, and of the unknown.

Medication helped with my recovery. Once I was back on my feet again, I began to explore ways in which I could broaden my experience, make new friends and learn to feel good about myself, all with the aim of attracting a lasting love. I signed up to Louise Hay's *Heal Your Life* class, and it changed my life. Our teacher told us to carefully choose three affirmations and recommended that we commit pen to paper three times a day, to engrave these positive affirmations in our subconscious minds. We were to write each affirmation ten times. There was something about writing them out that made them real and defined. I felt clarity, certainty, as I ticked the box at the end of each day. While reciting and singing the affirmations are also highly effective, I tended to focus on the written task. I would repeat it at various times over the course of the day, whenever I remembered the new life that I was creating for myself. With each positive affirmation, I was taking a step in the right direction.

Here are some affirmations to get you started. You can personalise them however you wish.

I believe with all my heart, soul and spirit, and with every ounce of my being, that a wonderfully loving man, my perfect match, will come into my life at the right moment. I await his arrival with anticipation and excitement.

*I deserve the love of an amazing man. As I believe
more with every day that I am divinely entitled to
a loving relationship, I draw him nearer.*

*I am the embodiment of love, honesty, kindness,
appreciation, respect, intelligence, stability, and more.
Therefore, I can attract only the same into my life.
Like attracts like. I attract what I am.*

*Affirmations empower me. They help me to feel hopeful.
Hopeful people expect love. I expect love. I receive what I
expect. I know that is true because it is a law of life. I look
around and see all the other people who expect love and
find it easily. I emulate them. I feel hopeful and expectant.*

STEP 4: Meditate and visualise

Meditation has provided me with an effective way to access peace and hope. Early on my journey, I began to practise a very intense and transformative type of meditation called Ananda Mandala, which involves intense breathing, comprising deep inhalation followed by sharp (at times painful) exhalation only through the nose. Although I always found it difficult and not at all relaxing, the feeling that washed over me upon completion is the closest I have come to experiencing euphoria. Less intense meditations, though not quite as physically or mentally demanding, have never brought me the same level of contentment as Ananda Mandala. While it is hard work, it is definitely worth doing and you'll reap benefits that exceed your wildest dreams.

I downloaded various meditation tracks to my iPod and set it up so that each track is followed by approximately 20 minutes of beautifully soothing music. During these moments of bliss, I would visualise my ideal relationship and picture how my life would look and feel if I were involved with a wonderful man. Imagining this possibility awakened in me a feeling of joy and excitement that I had not experienced since childhood. As a child, I had been a real daydreamer. This ability to lose myself in dreams of better times ahead lasted beyond my teenage years.

When you were a child, you believed that life had limitless potential. Every passing year seemed to diminish the capacity of your imagination to excite and enthral you. You gradually lost your ability to manifest an imaginary friend. By the time you reached your thirties, your vision of the future was limited to what was most likely to happen based on statistics generated by some government think-tank. If it is in your nature to see the glass as half-empty rather than half-full, you will think of all the women who remain single, even those more beautiful and charismatic than you are. No great love stories have ever been written on the back of facts and statistics. Meditation helps you to get out of the dark corners of your head, in which frightening statistics and horror stories lurk. Succumb to the power of your imagination, just as you did when you were a child, and let it fill you with excitement and hope.

Try not to be too specific in your visualisation of the man of your dreams. While you may be hoping that he will turn out to be the blonde guy you see on the bus every morning, it is best to focus instead on how you will feel in his presence. While you can visualise the setting in detail, your image of him should be amorphous, so that you'll remain open to various possibilities. Picture yourself sitting in a seat at the cinema. He has popped out to the popcorn stand to buy a bucket for the two of you to share. His coat is draped over the back of his chair. Inside the pocket, his phone beeps with a message from his sister who's wondering if he's with you. You smile warmly as he returns to his seat. He tells you something he just observed that he knows you will find amusing. You laugh together.

This is constructive daydreaming. You are using your mind like a magnet to attract your ideal man into your life. You are drawing him, and love, inexorably closer to you. Time and time again, I focused upon how it would feel to be in the company of someone with whom I could laugh and talk or share a companionable silence. Each day, I looked forward to my ritual of meditation followed immediately by visualisation. View it not as a chore but as a treat. It's an opportunity to attract true love.

Dreaming is a great and necessary step in creating a new and wonderful reality for yourself. Don't waste your time by dreaming about things that are impossible, unalterable or in the past, as you may lose heart if your desired outcome seems too far beyond your grasp. Dream about the best possible outcome for your situation. Unless you already happen to mix in Hollywood circles, dreaming of being swept off your feet by an award-winning actor is neither realistic nor helpful. Meeting a successful, smart man who appreciates and adores you is an attainable goal. Imagine how it would feel to be someone's number one—the person who's on their mind as soon as they wake up. Many people believe themselves to be undeserving of this perfectly realisable ambition.

I don't believe that any one of the steps I took was pivotal in bringing love to me. I view my journey as a holistic, integrated process. Becoming open to love and drawing love towards you requires building your confidence and sense of self-worth in many different ways and at many different levels. The primary ambition of each of the twenty steps was to strengthen my belief in my ability to attract love into my life.

Faith grows out of hope that is consistently cultivated. If you hope that love can be yours and you nurture this hope every day, this hopeful anticipation will gradually develop into a robust expectation that your future holds love. While some people are blessed with an unquestioning belief in their entitlement to a wonderful relationship, many of us have to work on it. This daily habit will strengthen your belief that love is rightfully yours. Be positive and patient as you wait for love to come to you.

STEP 5: Join a support group

Surround yourself with allies who will support and bolster you when you're feeling down or defeated. Joining a group of positive, encouraging, like-minded women is a wonderful way to motivate yourself to change. Each person is on their own journey, has their own challenges, and will progress at their own pace. I have found that friendships forged in these supportive environments are incredibly enriching and tend to last.

I enrolled in a wonderful *Heal Your Life* course based upon the teachings of Louise L. Hay. Over the course of the ten weeks, I became lifelong friends with the other women in the group and our instructor, Mary Kate. The exercises were incredibly cathartic. Together we laughed, cried, empathised, made changes, faced temporary setbacks, and planned our futures. Something very powerful happens when people come together with the shared aim of affecting positive change. Over the years, we have seen each other develop, learn and grow.

Mary Kate, a strong, free-spirited, creative woman, has lived the lessons that she taught us in the class. She guided us through gentle, life-affirming, enjoyable activities and challenges. In the words of Esther Hicks, everything was downstream, with the flow. We heard things that we had been programmed all our lives to dismiss. *Work can and should be fun. Love can be easy when it is with the right person in the right place and at the right time.* Mary Kate introduced me to the Ananda Mandala technique and set me on the path to love. To her I am deeply grateful.

When I began the course, I knew very little about Louise Hay and her philosophy. By the end of the first night, I was hooked. Hay taught that everything you think and say goes out into the world and comes back multiplied. She trusted that only good things lay ahead of her and made a habit of expressing gratitude for all the things that brought her joy. Through conducting mirror work, in which I looked at my reflection whilst repeating affirmations, I became aware of my resistance to hearing positive statements about myself. Acknowledging this self-rejection was the first step of the journey to self-acceptance. I was shocked to discover how little sympathy I was willing to give myself. I saw a pathetic little girl asking for something she would never receive. Observing the other group members as they, too, wrestled with self-doubt, I learned that each and every one of us has our struggles. The strength and encouragement I received from the other women helped me to stay positive and to find hope, even if at first it was only a glimmer.

STEP 6: Write a letter to Santa

In the early Noughties, I wrote a letter to the Universe requesting my ideal relationship. I was sceptical, as at that time I did not believe in a divine and organising force working behind the scenes on my behalf. I wrote a list of the physical and emotional qualities I was seeking in a partner and then released it into the wind, because I didn't want anyone to find it. Having no faith, I was completely detached from the process and it failed to ignite any excitement in me.

Whenever I contemplated meeting a man who I liked and would like me back, I immediately focused on how my life would turn out if this didn't happen. I pictured myself single, isolated and scared, and I became filled with anxiety. These daydreams were punitive and dispiriting, instead of exciting and inspiring.

I had noticed that certain people seem to always get what they want, whether or not they deserve it. Those people speak about their dreams and aspirations with a sense of inevitability. They speak of *when* and not *if*. They do not doubt that they have the ability to make their dreams materialise. No mental blocks hold them back. They don't hope for things, they expect them. I knew I needed to learn to feel expectancy.

That's how I came up with the idea of writing a letter to Santa. As a child, I had never doubted that I deserved to get what I wanted, so I never sold myself short when it came to my extensive list of demands. It was around Christmas, and although I no longer believe in Santa Claus, I thought writing to him might help me to remember what it feels like to request something and to believe that it will arrive within a given time. I knew that channelling this magical sense of faith, by returning to a concept linked with a time when hope was in abundance, might teach me to feel expectant once again. For the first time in a very long while, I began to feel that this could happen for me. I could meet a wonderful man. I was excited. I was very specific about what I was seeking, and I urge you to do the same but without limiting yourself.

By the time I posted my letter to Santa, the man I'd requested had already made an appearance in my life as Gilbert, but I hadn't yet recognised him as a potential partner. I had gone on one date with him and we'd been texting regularly ever since. By this time, I had been hurt quite badly by men playing games with me. Needing desperately to be in control, I had begun to play games as well. Especially if the man was nice, I would make him work incredibly hard, and I would refuse to initiate conversation. I wanted him to dance to my tune for the entire date.

I felt I had the upper hand with Gilbert, as he'd been eagerly texting me over the Christmas period to arrange a follow-up. In late

January, we went on a second date. I acted cold and nonchalant. The following morning, he didn't text me. I waited all day. When I finally received a text, it wasn't from him. It was from the guy I had previously been seeing, who had treated me badly. The crushing disappointment I felt was a huge wake-up call.

I sent Gilbert an obtuse text apologising for my rude behaviour. I have no idea why I thought that would prompt him to ask me out again, but it made perfect sense to me at the time. He texted me a lovely, sincere reply, telling me not to worry. My plan had backfired. He took my apology not as an invitation to try again but as an explanation for my rudeness and confirmation of my disinterest in him. Annoyed that he hadn't taken the bait, I deleted his number. We were still connected via Facebook, so I messaged him a few days later. I apologised for my behaviour and suggested another date, and he responded immediately, his tone reassuringly warm and enthusiastic. The subsequent dates were amazing and literally changed my life. As Marilla in Anne of Green Gables says, "There is a book of revelations in everyone's life." Mine was that I actually really liked this guy.

STEP 7: Ask your friends to set you up

At the end of 2011, shortly before Christmas, my father was giving me a lift to a housewarming party on the other side of the city from where I lived. I wasn't particularly looking forward to it, as I didn't expect to know anyone there except the hostess. I did not relish the prospect of making small talk with strangers all night. I told my father I was planning to stay for an hour and then get a taxi home. He reassured me that it might turn out to be the best night of my life. I was not too hopeful in that regard. To date, such nights had never proven life changing.

Upon arriving at the party, I was relieved to see some friendly faces from school. I ran into a girl I had always liked but hadn't seen in years. I told her all about the last guy I had dated, and she was appalled by his lack of grace and manners. I plucked up the courage to ask her whether she might introduce me to someone she knew. Before this, I had never thought of asking anyone to set me up. I'd had some bad experiences on blind dates, so I had long stopped considering them as an option. She borrowed her husband's phone and scrolled through his address book. They offered to set me up with Gilbert. They both sang his praises. It all sounded too good to be true. When she showed me his photo, I purposely squinted my eyes for fear of making a snap judgment and writing off another potentially wonderful partner.

Twenty-one months later, this couple were the first people outside our families we told of our engagement. My husband and I would never have met if I hadn't asked for their help and if they hadn't been willing to do it. So, please let it be known that you are willing to go on blind dates. And once you meet the love of your life, don't forget to pay the favour forward. I'm sure you know lots of wonderful men and women who would be eternally grateful for an introduction. A few years later, I set up two of my friends and they have since married and started a family.

STEP 8: Know that it can happen just like that

Much of what we believe about ourselves and our situations becomes a reality. If we don't believe in ourselves or our capacity to form healthy, loving relationships, this can be very limiting. The best thing a friend can do for you is to offer you their blind faith. Two friends of mine separately reassured me that they had no doubt whatsoever that I would meet someone special. It did wonders for my confidence, because for the first time in my life I felt as if someone really believed in my ability to find love. It is probably one of the nicest and most empowering things that you can do for a friend who despairs of meeting her ideal man. I was lucky enough to have two such friends. I recommend that you spend as much time as possible in the company of people who are blinded by your brilliance and not afraid to tell you.

Take heart when you see others settling into relationships, getting married, and having kids. Do not take comfort in the fact that other lonely people are in the same boat as you. Each friend, neighbour, relative or stranger who finds love is helping you to find it too. If they can do it, then you most certainly can. Hope is contagious, and you should do your best to catch it. When you have, make sure to pass it on! Don't get bogged down in the details of how, where and when you'll meet your perfect man. Just decide today to believe that your ideal man is making his way toward you.

Get out there and do things you enjoy. The happier you become, the more joy you'll radiate, attracting other joyful people into your life. Instead of joining a tennis club with the sole purpose of meeting a man, do it because it's fun. You will be far more interesting to yourself and others if you have diverse interests and a varied life. You won't be waiting around for your ideal man. He'll come and find you, as you are busy pursuing your interests and enjoying yourself. Be the type of person that you'd like to meet. Like attracts like. Interested people are interesting.

One of my friends from the Louise Hay class had read all of Wayne Dyer's books. She told me to avoid making the common mistake of meditating on what you want instead of *being what you wish to manifest*. It struck me as very profound. I should be the type of person I'd like to attract into my life. I understood that Dyer is suggesting that we endeavour to vibrate at the same emotional frequency as the type of people we want to attract as friends, partners or lovers.

I was becoming increasingly interested in the idea that thoughts are vibrations, and that the thoughts that we have are not confined to our interior minds. I wondered whether people could actually sense how little I valued myself. This would mean that the Universe was responding to my estimation of myself and presenting me with opportunities that were a vibrational match. It's not a matter of acting self-confident or faking it until you make it, but of cultivating those feelings within oneself. I would have to embody all the qualities I longed for in a relationship. I would have to *become* kindness, generosity, positivity, hope, expectation, humour and intelligence.

Instead of seeing obstacles where none existed, I began to envision the many opportunities awaiting me in the near future. Whenever I slipped back into my default negative and catastrophic style of thinking, I told myself that this new way of being in the world would pay off. I was surrounded by perfectly unexceptional and ordinary women, just like me, who had formed healthy relationships with men. (There is nothing wrong with the descriptors *unexceptional* and *ordinary*, if we accept that being a typical human being is pretty extraordinary in and of itself.) The only difference between us was that they had known all along how easy it is to meet a nice man and that it can happen just like that. I craved the self-belief that other ordinary women seemed to possess. When you have faith that the right man will present himself in your life at the right time and in the right place, you become less anxious, and you inevitably feel a lot happier. This is exactly when and how you will attract your ideal match. When I began to trust in a Higher Plan, I attracted my husband into my life. When I released the fear and anxiety around being single, I became a different person. The man I have attracted into my life is very different from the ones I attracted when I was fearful, negative and anxious.

It can happen just like that came from a friend on the Heal Your Life course. She was blessed with the mindset that it's easy to meet men. That had always been her experience. She had met her partner on their first night in college accommodation, when he had stopped by with his friends. I had always focused on negative things I'd heard and read: people don't meet in pubs or bars anymore; he won't just come knocking on your door; you won't meet your husband in a book shop. By the time I met my husband-to-be, I was on the way to becoming a very different person. I had released that old, limiting belief that it was hard to meet men. If you believe it is easy, then it is. It matters little whether you meet him via a dating app, on a blind date or at the bus stop.

STEP 9: Be modest

Truly attractive people radiate energy and presence. They don't need to sell themselves. Any effort at self-promotion would be needless and tacky. We all have met people who shower us with anecdotes that they hope will impress us, when it's clear that the person they most need to convince of their worth is themselves. This not someone to despise, but rather to pity. We all crave attention and validation at certain points in our lives, usually in those areas where we most lack confidence. Boasting makes us less likeable, especially to ourselves. If you seek acceptance and love from yourself and others, put self-promotion to one side. Whenever I try to impress others, I always feel embarrassed afterwards. Let others praise you; praising yourself just makes you feel worse in the long run. Decide what type of person you are, be that person and enjoy being her. If you were a luxury brand, would it be appropriate to advertise on TV shopping channels late at night? Again, it would be needless, tacky, and ultimately damaging to the brand. The next time you're at a dinner party wondering why no one is interested in you, bring your thoughts back to who you are at your best, who you enjoy being, and why you are wonderful. Realise what it is about you that makes you so interesting, special and different. Take note of how people's reactions to you change when you begin to radiate self-acceptance. It is powerful. You think, speak and carry yourself differently when you fully accept yourself in all your humanity.

I worked with a woman who had a wickedly funny sense of humour. She often talked about men checking her out. She would gaze seductively at them in her local bar, in the gym or on the train. She once arranged to have Fridays off in order to synchronise her schedule with that of a certain man, so they could spend as much time together as possible. By the time it turned out that he wasn't interested, she had become interested in someone else. When the gym instructor demonstrated kicks and punches on the bank of the swimming pool as she cycled on her stationary bike in the adjacent gym, she interpreted it as an attempt to impress her. When I told her that he was teaching an aqua-aerobics class, she said she knew when a man was going out of his way to gain her attention.

Even if men are competing for your attention, there is no need to let everyone know. Other women will like you less, and only very easily impressed men will be spurred on by the competition. If, like most insecure people, your boasting is an attempt to reassure yourself of your worth, realise that you are not doing yourself any favours. When you begin to gain greater self-awareness, you will note how deflated you feel following a bout of self-promotion. See how much better you feel when you resist the urge to brag. You will like yourself more as a result and others will mirror this back to you.

STEP 10: Embrace your unique qualities

Instead of trying to change the aspects that make you different, you might try to emphasise and celebrate them instead. If you have vibrant red hair, dying it blonde in an attempt to give yourself broader appeal may well achieve that end; but instead of attracting one man who thinks you're amazing, you may well attract five who think you're quite attractive. People who divide opinion tend to do better on dating sites because they highlight the qualities that make them stand out. There will be hundreds of quite attractive people logged on at any given time, but quite possibly only a few others will share the distinctive characteristic you possess—the one that makes you interesting and unusual. If you have pale, freckled skin, suspending yourself overnight in a vat of fake tan to achieve that bronzed glow may make you more appealing to the average man, but no more appealing than any of the other hundreds of girls who opt for this look. You should bear in mind that the men who adore freckles will be highly motivated to seek you out. Don't be afraid to be different. Being unusual makes you stand out.

Emphasise your differences, capitalise on them and make them work for you. You want a man who recognises your unique beauty and doesn't fall for you only once you have erased all signs of your individuality. If you believe that your true self isn't good enough for him in the first place, you will like yourself less, feel less secure, and grow to resent him in the long run.

My red hair has a strawberry blonde hue, which tends to lighten somewhat in the summer. In my twenties, whenever someone described me as having blonde hair, I was secretly chuffed. This wasn't because I wanted to have blonde hair—I could have very easily dyed my hair any number of shades, but because I recognised the intrinsic power in being part of a group that was considered naturally more attractive and undeniably more popular with men.

I became friends with Margaret when we were teaching in a substitute capacity in a secondary school. We were both single and felt terribly lonely and rudderless. Even though we were only in our very early thirties, we feared that we would soon find it too hard to meet a decent, available man. Margaret advised me to dye my hair blonde, as she strongly believed that men were biologically predisposed to find blonde hair attractive. She assured me that once the person had fallen in love with me, I could always go back to red. Many other friends had voiced the same opinion.

Even at my lowest point, I didn't want to be with the type of man that would be attracted to me only after I'd obliterated a perfectly acceptable element of my appearance. Yet my fear of ending up alone was greater than my sense of self, and I followed her advice to some degree by highlighting my hair. At first, it was a subtle adjustment that was noticed only by my most perceptive friends and acquaintances, but over the next two years of regular salon visits, the portion of highlighted hair increased until my hair was predominantly blonde. My hair was starting to remind me of an Easi Single. Even at my blondest, I wasn't a bombshell, but I feared that returning to red would render me completely invisible to men. So I resisted my instincts and decided to stick with a colour that did nothing for me, just to secure the attention I received on occasion from men in whom I was invariably not interested. I reckoned that if I was unpopular as a blonde, I would be a complete write-off as a redhead.

After discovering that the man I was seeing already had a girlfriend and wasn't the slightest bit interested in me, I decided to take the plunge. I went back to red, the colour I liked best and which suited me most. It wasn't about the colour of my hair; it was about being comfortable with myself and not living my life according to my perception of what other people liked.

STEP 11: Raise your standards

Casting a wider net means being open to people and experiences you might have never previously considered. But this should never mean lowering your standards. At one time or another, we all have sold ourselves short and reaped the consequences. Dating is another area in which letting your standards slide leads to unhappiness in the long run. You should date only the type of man that would meet your best friend's approval.

If you're not attracted to the men you are dating or if the men you approach on dating websites tend to skip over your profile and ignore your messages, you might consider that they are not in your league. While you may be tempted to lower your standards; please consider raising them instead.

Many women feel more confident approaching men they don't find physically attractive, because they see them as a safer bet. In my experience, you cannot predict how anyone will behave judging purely by their physical appearance. Don't rule out someone or assume they won't be attracted to you simply because you find them conventionally attractive. The fact that you're attracted to them bodes well. Until you get to know them, you won't know what their tastes or preferences might be or how they might treat you.

Eve, a friend of a friend, had lived in Ireland for thirty-five years. Because she tended to pursue men who weren't interested in her, and to date men who didn't meet her standards, she'd had many relationships but none of them had lasted. Almost immediately after moving to the States for work, she met a man who is just as amazing as she is. They married and she gave birth to their first child two years (to the day) after their first encounter.

You won't feel good about making a lifetime commitment to some-one who is not truly matched with you. Deep down, you'll always feel that you don't belong together. Even though well-intentioned friends and relatives may tell you that you're being too picky and that you'll price yourself out of the market, stay strong and main-tain your standards. Be discerning; but be careful that you do not write off a perfectly nice man upon first sight.

One Monday morning, a colleague told me she had gone to a rugby match at the weekend with a large group of friends. After the match, they went on to a nightclub, where she ended up talk-ing to the brother of one of her friends. He was a lovely guy who showed great interest in her work, but she left the conversation to chat to a different guy, who spoke at length about his ambi-tion to become a pro skateboarder. As he was talking, a bouncer came over and yanked the skater from his stool and bundled him out through the fire exit. I was struck by the fact that she spent much of our conversation speculating on what had happened to the drunken braggart, instead of being concerned that she had shunned a decent, handsome man who had seemed genuinely interested in her.

You might want to think twice about choosing the showy, arrogant guy over the sweet, decent guy who tries hard and is nice. Go on a few dates with the sweet guy and see what happens; he may surprise you. Model looks become boring after a while, if there's nothing else to back them up. Gilberts have a tendency to become more attractive the more you get to know them, and never under-estimate the power of sexual chemistry. Give the sweet guys a chance, and one of them may turn out to be your very own Gilbert Blythe. It worked for me!

STEP 12: Keep seeing him (unless he is a loser)

If you are like me and a lot of other women, it may take you some time to figure out whether you find someone attractive. Someone who fails to make a blip on your radar might command your attention a few days later, after making some subtle alteration to his appearance, such as wearing a different coat. Don't rule someone out just because he isn't your usual physical type. Unless there is something wholly objectionable about him, there is a chance that he will grow on you. In your eyes, he may become the most attractive man alive. If you are not initially attracted to someone, it may just be a question of time until you acquire a taste for them. Once you get there, the attraction may run that much deeper or be all the more layered than if you had instantly felt it. It may last a lifetime.

When I met my husband for the first time, I found him to be a very pleasant-looking man but didn't consider him my type. A month later, we went on our second date. By that time, he had really grown on me. He showed up for our third date with a new haircut, and I was sold! Do not underestimate the power of a nice haircut.

Unless there is nothing at all you like about a man, go on a couple of dates with him before making up your mind. That being said, certain behaviours are unacceptable. If your date spends the evening checking out other women, he has proven to you that he is a womaniser. Don't see him again. Be glad that he has shown his true colours early on.

I spent far too many years giving second chances to all the wrong types of men. I went on a date with a man who intermittently gawked at one other woman all night. After a well-meaning friend convinced me that this behaviour had been a figment of my imagination, I reluctantly agreed to a second date. He spent the entire evening openly eyeing up every woman in the bar. It seemed he'd been on his best behaviour on our first date. It was as if his head were on a swivel. He leaned back on his barstool at one point to get an eyeful of someone else's date. I felt that he was treating me with disrespect, but others assured me that a lot of men behaved this way and that I shouldn't take it personally. I had been single for a long time and had lost perspective on which kinds of behaviour I should find acceptable. My niece's christening was fast approaching. Even though I wasn't planning to invite him, my mind flashed on an image of him leering at all of my female relatives. At that moment, I understood that my instincts had been spot-on. I deleted his number from my phone and decided I would ignore his texts. I should have trusted my instincts from the outset. As Maya Angelou wrote: *When someone shows you who they are, believe them.*

In college, I was friends with a guy who spent a long time mooning over an insipid girl who wasn't interested in him but clearly enjoyed the attention. Turned off by this delusional behaviour, I had never been attracted to him, although some of my friends thought he was cute. More than five years later, we reconnected via Facebook. For months, he drunkenly texted me that a date with him would be one to remember. At the time, my confidence was at rock bottom, so I forgave him his obsession with the vapid girl and agreed to meet him for a drink after work one summer evening.

Our date was memorable, but for all the wrong reasons. He made inappropriate comments about a few of our mutual friends and sought a lot of reassurance about his appearance. He tried to pass off a well-known Woody Allen quotation as his own and threw a few insults my way for good measure.

I realised he was one of those men who knew how to spot a weak and vulnerable woman. He was unavailable, which made me think I liked him more than I did. Had he been available, I would have had to really consider what being in a relationship with a sleazy, manipulative, cheap and insecure man would be like. Boredom, fear and low self-esteem had brought me to a point where I was willing to indulge someone I didn't trust or like. It was an utterly demeaning experience, for which I am grateful because it allowed me to appreciate and accept the love of the good man who appeared in my life some years later.

STEP 13: Resist the urge to criticise

When I was younger, it used to really irk me whenever a person whose appearance I considered plain or ordinary was described as beautiful. On the other hand, if I thought someone was beautiful, I didn't mind others acknowledging it. They were simply affirming what I already knew to be true. Having always been a good student, I felt secure in that aspect of my life, so I would never begrudge anyone compliments or praise about academic achievements. But because I had experienced such raging insecurity about my appearance while growing up, it angered me when people received what I felt were unwarranted compliments about their appearance. Why should anyone else feel good about themselves when I felt so awful?

Compelled to voice my opinion, I became irritated when others did not concur. Why should someone else's opinion of another person's appearance matter so much to me? I was always daydreaming about how I might restructure my face and body. I visited plastic surgeons, seeking outcomes that were unrealistic. I viewed others through harsh and unforgiving eyes because that was how I viewed myself.

Over the years, even as my confidence grew, I continued to feel uneasy about my appearance. Certain situations brought me straight back to childhood, when insensitive relatives had showered my sisters with compliments and I had felt ashamed for not being pretty enough. My insecurities would rise to the surface and I would be compelled to voice my disagreement with someone on the matter of another person's beauty. After one such occasion a number of years ago, I awoke the following morning feeling embarrassed by the words I'd used to describe another woman. The person who was pushing my buttons had insecurities of her own. In disagreeing with her, I felt that I was putting her in her place, but all I was really doing was showing the world just how unhappy I was with myself.

On the back of that experience, I decided that I wanted to be a different type of person. After that, whenever I found myself in similar anxiety-provoking situations, I imagined that I was just as confident about my looks as I was about my brainpower. It took practice, and I wasn't always able to bite my tongue, but I learned not to voice my disagreement. As time went on, I stopped minding it so much. As I grew less critical of others, I became less critical of myself. I began to like parts of myself that I'd previously hated. Nothing is more attractive than someone who readily accepts herself and others just as they are.

The danger of judging other people is that it fills your mind with negativity and toxic emotions, which poison your outlook. Worst of all, you won't see the damage accrue. Before long, you'll be a misanthrope who scoffs and sneers at anyone who thinks, looks or sounds differently to you. Being uptight and critical is an obstacle to finding love. It will be harder to find love with a loving and gentle person if you only ever display your critical or self-righteous self. While it's perfectly admirable to have strong feelings about issues that are close to your heart, we all know that person who seems to enjoy getting thoroughly exercised about matters. Having a sense of justice is a fine thing but not at the expense of your sense of fun. Balance is key. Most of us have one or two areas where we need to lighten up and loosen up. Don't be the person that your friends would hesitate to set up on blind dates, because, despite your physical allure and natural charm, you are too much like hard work. Adopt a kind and generous outlook, and you will find a man with a similar view on the world.

STEP 14: Trust your instincts

It can be tempting to defer to other people's opinions when you are feeling unsure of yourself; but consistently ignoring your instincts will serve only to erode your self-belief. By abdicating responsibility for your life decisions, you stand to lose much more than you would if you simply made the wrong call once in a while. Any discomfort you may experience in the short term will be outweighed by the boost in confidence you will gain by learning to call the shots in your own life.

You can start with the small things. Stop asking other people if it's cold outside, what you should wear, whether you should get a bus or a taxi to the concert, which dish is less fattening. Expert advice is invaluable when making decisions that involve a lot of money, time and effort; however, you are perfectly capable of deciding which route to take to work, if you should get highlights in your hair, and whether you can afford a new car. There is nothing less attractive than a person who becomes paralysed by simple decisions, who flits from one person to the next, soliciting advice yet not heeding it, as they are too busy thinking of what the next person might have to say on the matter.

Once, a colleague rang me up to ask me how she should prepare for her end-of-term exams. She was studying for a postgraduate qualification in a subject I know nothing about. I knew even less about her learning style, her sleeping rhythms and her preferred study patterns. She rattled off a string of options: should she study early or late, at home or in the library, before or after the gym, by writing or recitation, and so on. She was so terrified of failing that she sought advice from someone whose only qualification was not being her. She just didn't want to be the one in control.

Today you can start thinking for yourself. Start by making small, day-to-day decisions. You will feel more independent and you will respect yourself more. This is important if you wish to attract someone into your life who respects themselves as well as you. This may seem not to relate directly to the topic of romance, but your relationship with yourself is, and always will be, your primary relationship. Focus on this relationship and make it as strong as it can be.

STEP 15: Say goodbye to negative friends

Kristina and I were friends for five years, when we were in our twenties. She was an amazing laugh and possessed a sharp wit and a droll sense of humour, along with lashings of undiluted nastiness. I accepted her, in all her thinly veiled wickedness, because I found her interesting. We had similar views and disliked, and disapproved of, the same people. Her sarcasm wasn't tempered with anything resembling kindness. She had no soft centre. She would quite happily put herself down if it meant that she could take me down with her. She didn't need friends, which was just as well, as she didn't have many. It wasn't that she was unpopular, but she disposed of friends as if they were plastic cutlery. At the time, I was her only reliable and constant friend. I was the encouraging, kindly, supportive friend she criticised and derided, all with a wry smile. She was a highly offensive person who claimed to be highly sensitive. I was lonely at the time and didn't feel all that positive about myself, so I was willing to tolerate unacceptable behaviour.

One afternoon, after I had spent hours listening to her describe how cruelly her family treated her, she recommended that I rent a classic Eighties romcom called *Pretty in Pink*. She quickly filled me in on the plot, but I was pretty sure that I'd seen it before. She referred to the movie's lead—the gorgeous, russet-haired Molly Ringwald—as the underdog. She said that in real life things just wouldn't happen like that. The redhead would never get the guy. It was such a transparent attempt to provoke my insecurity. Her words failed to achieve their desired impact; what upset me was that someone who claimed to be my friend would so desperately try to hurt me. In that moment, I saw her as she really was. I glared at her with pure dislike and disregard before flouncing off. I ignored her texts for a while. But with low self-esteem being what it is and loneliness my biggest dread, I accepted her back into my life.

Not long after that, she dispensed with me, just as she did with any of her friends who said the wrong thing. I committed the cardinal sin of trying to reassure her that she was not ugly, by saying what I believed to be true—that she was an unconventional beauty. In that instant, the door to that friendship was unceremoniously slammed shut. As it was not the desired response, I was ushered out the door of her life. She had so much going for her, but she was so consumed by hatred that she cut herself off from the world and hurt those who cared for her the most. My world is now filled with friends who couldn't be more different from her. We build each other up instead of tearing each other down. Friends who try to hurt you are not your friends! It's as simple as that.

I also lost a new friend by failing to act with integrity. Shortly after we met, she began to call me frequently to discuss her emotional woes. Feeling annoyed, I vented my frustration in a text to a different friend and fired it off. Two seconds later I realised I had sent the text to the friend about whom I was complaining. Then, instead of handling it with grace, I sent her a shoddy excuse. She returned by post a Dr Phil book on finding love that I had lent her some months earlier. I later sent a message of apology, but I'm not sure whether she received it. Be a good friend if you can. Vow today to nurture supportive friendships.

STEP 16: See yourself through an admirer's eyes

Some people adore each other with a level of devotion that defies reason. That's what's so amazing about love, it transcends logic. I had always assumed that the more ordinary the man, the greater the chance of his adoring me. Therefore, as a rule, I readily plumped for wholly unexceptional men. Fortunately for me, I discovered in time that the more exceptional the man, the more exceptional his love. If a man hasn't cared enough to cultivate kindness and generosity within himself, he is unlikely to appreciate those fine qualities in you. When you listen to certain songs or read certain poems, you can imagine how the artist sees his beloved. You almost begin to see her through his eyes. Love is complex. It is nuanced and immeasurable, and particular to each person and their ideals of love, beauty and friendship. It is wonderful how someone who is utterly unappealing to me might be the love of another person's life. When you listen to a song you love, imagine that this song was written about you. Imagine a wonderful man thinking of you whenever he hears this song. Picture him seeing you in his mind's eye. Visualise him adoring you. Experience what that feels like in your heart.

When I was in my twenties, I would listen to "She's Got A Way" by Billy Joel and visualise myself through the eyes of someone who adored me. I did this every time I played it on my iPod or heard it on the radio. Shortly after I met my husband, we went off to the West of Ireland for a few days. I brought a Billy Joel CD for the car journey. By the time we reached our destination, my husband-to-be had picked out that particular song as his favourite. He said it reminded him of me. He would later suggest it as the song for the first dance at our wedding.

This is a small thing you can do, listening to a song and imagining someone else thinking of you. When I did it, it awoke in me the sense of possibility. Music, like any form of art, can open the soul in ways that cogent argument cannot. Feeling that love is yours for the taking enlivens the spirit, making you instantly more attractive and drawing positive loving experiences in. If it makes you feel good and it keeps you hopeful, then do it!

STEP 17: Take the VIP Challenge

Let's do something fun together. Make yourself a nice cup of tea or cocoa. Locate a piece of paper and a pen. Now, imagine you've been assigned the task of taking care of a VIP for one day. You will have to do your best to impress this individual, to cater to their needs and to make sure that they feel contented and relaxed in your home. You really want this person to go home feeling great. You don't have to spend any extra money making this special person feel valued. You should concentrate all your energy on making a meaningful connection with this person and making them feel comfortable and respected in your presence. Plan out the day. You might want to write down your suggested activities and treats. Make a note of the things they might need.

You are a very important person—a VIP. Devote one day to carrying out the plans you've made. Treat yourself exactly as you had planned to treat your guest. At the end of the day, compose comprehensive feedback on your experience of being a guest in your life. What was good? What was not so good? Which areas might be improved? Keep your notes for future reference.

One month later, repeat The VIP Challenge. You might want to begin by looking at your plan and your guest feedback from one month ago. Make a new plan and devote one day to carrying it out. At the end of the day, compose your feedback.

Compare the two experiences. Did you implement any of your feedback from the first time? Did you feel better taken care of the second time around? Is there anything about this experience that you would like to take away from this day? Might you continue to treat yourself as you would a welcome guest in your home and in your life?

Even if you can show yourself a little bit more compassion on just one occasion over the course of the day, let yourself off the hook just once, you will have made excellent progress. It's all about treating yourself as you deserve to be treated. Start engaging with yourself in a respectful and loving manner, and other people will mirror that behaviour. It's not about demanding respect or expecting others to change their ways; it's about letting people treat you in whatever way they see fit and deciding for yourself whether or not that is good enough for you. There is no need to resort to sarcasm or putdowns when addressing your concerns. If someone is rude or abrupt in their dealings with you, simply state how you would prefer to be spoken to in future. While you cannot force anyone else to show you respect, you can treat yourself with respect.

STEP 18: Have a good laugh

After you've been sidelined, red-carded or fouled by that guy you didn't even fancy in the first place, you can spend the next week moping about how much of a loser you must be; deactivate your dating profile as an expression of your disgust with the entire male population; and vow never to hope again for the possibility of finding love. But where's the fun in that? Why punish yourself? If your niece or nephew came home from school in tears, after having been excluded in the playground by some of the more outgoing or confident children, would you poke them in the eye and tell them how you can see why they don't fit in, throw in a few insults and stand on their toe for good measure, before ignoring them for the rest of the day?

It can take some time to turn around your negative thinking after being rejected. It's unrealistic and unhealthy to put pressure on yourself to bounce back without any period of wound-licking. But in the meantime, you can let in a bit of light. Was there anything vaguely humorous about the situation? Life, love and relationships can be absurd. At times, they can even be ridiculous. You have to be willing to laugh at yourself and at the situation. Whatever the dating disaster, however dejected you may feel, try and wring a few laughs out of it.

Many years ago, I corresponded briefly with a French guy on a dating website before agreeing to meet him in person. On our date, he was incredibly self-important and a bit dull, and some of his remarks could have been construed as offensive. After the first drink, I made my excuses and left. In the days following, I didn't hear back from him, which didn't surprise me. Two weeks later, he texted me, asking me to join him for dinner in his apartment. I was quite taken aback. I didn't want to go, but I allowed a friend to talk me into giving him another chance. I had been obsessing over a different guy, one who was not reciprocating my interest. She said it would boost my confidence to be around someone who was interested in me.

On the night in question, just as I was about to leave for his place, I texted him to ask for directions. His swift reply, expressing surprise at my needing directions, momentarily threw me. Why wouldn't I need directions? Then it dawned on me. He thought that I'd been to his apartment before. After a few more texts, it became apparent that he had contacted the wrong Penelope. I was so relieved at not having to spend the evening with him that I jumped up and down in delight in my sitting room. Can you imagine if I had arrived at the door with a bottle of wine in hand, only to see by the look on his face that I was not the guest he'd been expecting? That would have been mortifying. But that little story has provided a lot of laughter over the years, giving me far more pleasure than any wallowing would have done.

If you are sitting around with your friends analysing the motivations of a man who has not yet gotten around to asking you out despite having multiple opportunities, you are wasting your time and theirs. Without realising it, you're depleting your store of self-respect and testing your friends' patience. You can be sure that they are beyond exasperated with you at this point. Don't be this person! I have been the annoying friend on some occasions and the irritated listener on others. Be a source of joy, someone your friends look forward to seeing. Do not be that crazy girl who makes every conversation into a monologue about some guy who will never ask her out. Only tell dating stories if they make your friends laugh.

Some of my friends have an amazing talent for turning dating debacles into hilarious morning-after text sessions. One of the greatest laughs I have ever had was with a friend of mine who was a serial dater. In a club the previous night, she had met a guy who she proudly described as a member of the defence forces. She said he was very nice and drove a decent car, but he had a hole in his chin. Her description was so graphic and her reaction so emotional that I assumed this was an injury sustained in a work-place accident. After much discussion, it became evident that this disfigurement was merely a dimple. We laughed, she moved on, and we swapped many other dating stories over the years. She eventually met a wonderful man who proposed to her within three months of their first meeting. He was the right man and it was the right time. They are still happily married and have three beautiful sons. And while the details of most of the anecdotes we exchanged have long been forgotten, the laughs we shared have not.

STEP 19: Treat yourself to a makeover (or lots of them!)

While it isn't necessary to make radical changes, you might want to get yourself a fringe, try out a new hair colour or tone up by joining a Pilates class, if you feel that any of these changes will boost your confidence. Dress up for the office, even if there are no eligible men working there. When you start to feel more attractive, you will begin to carry yourself differently. When you treat your appearance as if it matters and take the time to style your hair, get a manicure or groom yourself in a way that makes you look your best, people will mirror this back to you. They will start to regard you as someone attractive and pay you a little more respect and attention. People respond well to others who take care of themselves. Play around with affirmations that build your confidence. In the morning, as you are fixing your hair or applying your make-up, you might say:

> *I see myself through loving eyes as a beautiful,*
> *unique woman and the world now reflects*
> *that new reality back to me.*

Always remain true to yourself. Be the best version of you, rather than a poor imitation of someone else. You are unique; emphasise your distinctive qualities. Be your best, most confident self. When I was struggling with an eating disorder, I saw a therapist who recommended that I take a new photo of myself for my dating profile. She advised me to apply fake tan, wear something glittery, and pout. This look might have worked really well for someone else, but as she was asking me to erase everything that was original and unique about me, it would have sent a very strong and clear message, to myself and the men on that site, that I was not good enough as I was, and that I needed to conceal or change myself. I prefer to enhance my natural beauty, to build on what I already have. I wanted to attract the type of man who would appreciate my type of beauty, inside and out. I smiled politely as I agreed to give her suggestion a try. On my way out, I winced as she assured me that she really did think I could be *reasonably* attractive if I made a little more effort. In those days, it took me a lot longer to recover from insensitive remarks. Today, I will mull them over for only so long before brushing them off and focusing instead on a compliment someone has paid me.

No amount of newfound attention and compliments in the here and now can make up for a lifetime of low self-esteem. If you have long believed or been made to believe that you are unattractive and that you are unworthy of love, you will likely struggle to start believing that you are beautiful. But you would likely struggle with this even if the entire population of your hometown had voted you a ten out of ten in the looks department and held the score cards up for all to see every time you paraded through the town. Each of us battles with different issues. Getting a new hairstyle, finding the perfect foundation or having ten men simultaneously pursue you will not provide the validation that you sought when you were growing up. But accepting that you need to work on feeling positive and confident about your appearance is a liberating realisation.

STEP 20: Draw a picture of yourself with your future partner

Which activities do you most look forward to enjoying as part of a couple? When you picture yourself and your ideal man doing something really fun and romantic, what are you doing? Are you kayaking in an exotic location? Perhaps you're lying on a beach somewhere or enjoying a candlelit dinner for two. Or are you cuddling on the sofa in your PJs? Really submerge yourself into this scenario. Are you smiling yet? How do your mind and your heart feel?

Now, draw the picture of you and your future partner that you have just imagined. Because you've already pictured it so clearly in your mind, the drawing doesn't have to be incredibly accurate to remind you of the image and the sensation you've just experienced. A cartoon or sketch will do just fine, and this will leave you a lot of room to keep visualising your future partner without getting bogged down with specifics. Display the drawing where you will see it every day—perhaps above the bathroom mirror or on your bedroom door.

While I enjoyed doing this, I might have enjoyed it even more had I given myself free rein to create a colourful, fun image. My approach was far too serious—I sketched the image of myself from a photograph. I'd encourage you to take a looser approach and really enjoy the process.

Perhaps you can enlist your niece or nephew as your personal portrait artist. Ask them to draw the picture to your specifications and proudly display it on your fridge. Every time you look at it, you will be filled with a positive, hopeful feeling about the future.

Dating Intel

I'd like to share with you all of the things I wish someone had told me when I was dating. Actually, it's possible that people tried to pass on some of this advice but I was too focused on myself and stressed out about my situation to take it on board, let's just say these are the things I wish I had known.

This dating intel comes from my years of therapy and of reading every self-help book I could possibly get my hands on, from late-night conversations with friends (and their friends) who have been both lucky and unlucky in love, and my own experiences. I hope you'll treat these bits and bobs of hard-won advice as precious jewels handed from one woman to another. While every journey is unique, my hope is that these dating hacks will save you time and energy as you find your way to that perfect love.

Take pleasure in the anticipation

Now that you've absorbed all of this advice and implemented positive changes in your outlook and behaviour, you may be thinking, *I've put in all the work. I want to see results!* Even though you may be growing impatient, frustrated or despondent, this is not the time to get annoyed and give up, throw your hands in the air, and resign yourself to the lonely life of the perpetual singleton. You have likely done this before, so this is the time to try something else.

Push aside your feelings of annoyance and disappointment and create a positive headspace. You'll be far more likely to attract love when you are excited and hopeful. Draw that amazing man towards you and welcome him with open arms when he appears. Instead of dwelling on the fact that this wonderful man has yet to appear in your life, believe that great happiness lies ahead and take pleasure in anticipating what is to come. You are waiting for something that *will* happen, and that's a great position to be in. Allow yourself to feel the excitement.

You're waiting, but you are not in stasis. You are always moving toward your future. If you can stop focusing on the destination and start to enjoy the journey, the time will pass a lot more quickly because you'll be having so much fun. Sooner than you know it, your dreams will manifest. You truly believe with all your soul that a wonderful man will be yours. That's why you do not need to rush the process. Just as you enjoy the weeks leading up to Christmas every bit as much as the day itself, you can anticipate his arrival with joy and pleasure.

If a man says he doesn't believe in marriage, he doesn't (and he never will)

Most men will tell you quite clearly if they are incapable of committing to a relationship, but sometimes we don't hear it. When your potential life partner expresses his views on marriage, fidelity and children, listen closely and pay attention. These point to his core values, which are unlikely to change. If these values differ from yours, it is time to stop planning a future with him. If he tells you he has issues with commitment, cut your losses, run a mile, and don't look back.

Don't make the mistake of thinking you can change him; you can't. He is an adult, so if he has not reached an adequate level of maturity by this point in his life, it's unlikely to ever happen. It's not your job to raise him. If you stay with a man like this, your entire relationship will be a battle to convince him to change his values. You cannot force another person to settle down. Unless a committed relationship is something he already wants and is actively seeking, he's not the right guy for you.

Even when such a man makes a commitment due to external pressure or an ultimatum, his heart will not be in it, so he won't necessarily be faithful. Don't waste even one minute of your life trying to persuade him that you're worth changing for, because this is not about your *value*—it's about his *values*. It is not your job to win the debate or hoodwink him into marrying you. You do not want to be with a person like this. End it now, so you can free up time and space for a real relationship.

My friend Julie told me she'd heard a talk given in Vancouver by Oprah Winfrey's mentor, Iyanla Vanzant, in which she'd said that you can't demand that someone love you in a particular way. I searched online and found the recording. Her message was succinct. To paraphrase, she suggested that you observe how your partner treats you and decide whether you want to participate. If you are in an abusive or unhealthy relationship, it's easy to feel powerless. She places the onus on you to reclaim your power instead of abdicating responsibility. *You decide* whether you want to be part of a relationship that demeans and disempowers you.

Stop analysing your feelings

If you are wracking your brain about whether or not you really like a particular guy, chances are: you do. If you didn't, you wouldn't be spending hours each day trying to gauge the exact measure of your love and affection for him. But thinking about it is unlikely to give you an accurate reading. Only your heart can reliably tell you whether or not this man is the love of your life or has the potential to be. What you're doing is rather like looking up a Russian word in a French dictionary. Stop looking for answers where you will never find them. You won't be present in the relationship if you are all up in your head. Relax. Take some time out. Visualise yourself putting away the dictionary for the time being. Try to be in the moment and let things develop organically.

Shortly after meeting the man who was to become my husband, though I didn't know it yet, I went through a crisis of confidence similar to what you may experience in the near future. My sister casually said I could always end it if I didn't really like him. I was shocked by her suggestion. My mind raced: *I would never—could never do that. I like him far too much.* That's when I realised how I really felt about him. On another occasion, plagued by obsessive worrying thoughts, I fell asleep. Dreaming I had lost the love and affections of my partner, I cried out and sobbed uncontrollably. When I woke up to find it was just a dream, I felt a tremendous sense of relief. These two experiences galvanised my feelings and made them apparent to me. Faced with these scenarios, I had reacted so strongly that it was impossible to deny the extent and depth of my feelings for him.

Once you stop analysing your relationship to death, you'll be able to feel and to trust your emotions. You have greater control over your dreams than you imagine. As you drift off to sleep, you might try gently suggesting to yourself that you will dream about a particular topic. It's a fun, relaxing and creative way to tune into your emotions and let them help you to explore these questions, and it has often worked for me.

Before you fall asleep at night, fill your mind with positive thoughts and picture your dreams as having already manifested. Wayne Dyer recommends that we practise this visualisation technique for five minutes before slipping off into our unconscious state. The drowsy mind is highly suggestible, and when we see something in our mind as having already materialised, the universe will move mountains to replicate this image in reality. I very much looked forward to this nightly ritual. I would wait until I felt that sleep was close by, and then I would create delightful images in my mind of myself and my dream man in different situations: in the cinema, chatting easily as we waited for the film to start, at the airport, getting out our boarding passes; on the plane, exchanging bemused looks at a fellow passenger kicking up a fuss. All of these were very ordinary situations that I knew I would find myself in one day. I enjoyed seeing myself experiencing these everyday situations with someone special, who made me feel special. I always pictured a more relaxed version of myself, even though I have a tendency to become anxious when I travel. I knew that my perfect man would be a laidback individual who would bring a sense of calm to everything. Through my visualisation, I gained valuable insights about myself and what I needed and wanted from a relationship. When you are daydreaming or sleeping, theta brainwaves are dominant, and the mind is highly suggestible. There is no better time to plant in your subconscious the image of your desires made manifest.

Do not make him the centre of your world

Unless you have children, your world shouldn't revolve around anyone but yourself. By placing yourself at the centre of your world, you are not being selfish or egotistical. You are prioritising your needs so that you can best serve your life's purpose and be a source of strength for others, just as in an aeroplane emergency, you are to put on your oxygen mask before you attempt to help anyone else.

Give generously of your time. Helping other people is as much a balm for your soul as it is for theirs. There is no greater joy than providing comfort for someone in their time of need. The very act of serving others nourishes us. As an added bonus, the less time you spend ruminating on your own issues, the happier you will be. The more content you are, the more attractive you will appear to others.

When you meet someone special, you'll be excited about seeing him, but don't leave your friends high and dry so that you can devote all your time to him. Your friends deserve better, having stuck with you through thick and thin. As far as your new man is concerned, you won't be doing yourself any favours, as he will think you don't have very much going on in your life. Continue living your life to the fullest. Make space for your new man in your life, but not to the detriment of your other relationships. Don't drop everything and cancel your plans with family or friends because you've received a last-minute call from a love interest. You and the other people in your life deserve more respect than that.

If you and this man are joined at the hip, you will never have any stories to relay to him about your life outside of the relationship. You will become extensions of one another, and your world will become ever smaller. The purpose of letting someone into your life is to enrich your experience on this earth, not to let him become your entire world. You are two separate individuals, each having their own life. Maintaining a strong sense of yourself will keep you independent and interesting, and this will help the relationship to thrive in the long term.

Many years ago, I was helping my cousin prepare for an oral examination. Halfway through our study session, I received a text. It was from a man I had been seeing. We'd been on two rather underwhelming dates so far. A month had passed, and he was now requesting a third date. Despite my ambivalence, I suggested meeting up the following Saturday. We kept texting, and it soon came to light that he was requesting my company on that very night. I am ashamed to say that I dropped everything and cut the lesson short. My aunt gave me a lift back to my apartment so I could change and reapply my makeup before hotfooting it down to the local pub.

Needless to say, it was a disastrous encounter. He waved drunkenly to me as I approached the table at which he was slumped, and I knew I had made an egregious error. When I mentioned I'd been helping my cousin prepare for an upcoming exam, he tutted his disapproval and advised me not to give up my spare time to help others in future, assuring me he'd never made that mistake. He then announced that he had cheated on all of his previous girl-friends and that infidelity was harmless as long as you didn't rub your partner's nose in it. He told me a long and detailed story of how he'd convinced a friend to leave her long-term boyfriend for him, only to cheat on her the following weekend at a stag party in Scotland. I have always drawn the line at cheating. I was particu-larly appalled by the way he seemed to think he was some kind of great boyfriend because he'd felt a smidgeon of guilt afterwards. Though we didn't meet for another date, he continued to send me inappropriate messages for a year and a half afterwards.

I could have avoided this entire debacle if I'd seen what should have been apparent from the outset. He'd waited an entire month since our last date before asking me out at extremely short notice. Any man who does not request your company well in advance of a potential date does not respect you and does not deserve the gift of your time. Such a man is best avoided altogether. On this occasion, I did not show myself the respect I deserved, and I let myself and my cousin down. You should always set boundaries and honour them. Doing so keeps the wrong men out of your life. When you meet the one who's right for you, he'll respect your boundaries and recognise them as a sign that you respect yourself.

Do not spend too much time or money getting ready for a date

I once went speed dating with a woman who wore a ball gown to the event. Needless to say, she went home very disappointed. Spending too much time on your hair, face or outfit can reek of desperation. Having your make-up professionally applied is an unnecessary expense for any date. You will feel as if you are trying too hard, and the man you are meeting will perceive you as being overly-eager. A nice man will be complimented by your having made an effort, you do not need to wear a full face of foundation, false eyelashes and your best dress to secure his affection. If he likes you, he will do so regardless of whether you're slathered in makeup. He'll probably like you even more if you seem comfortable in your own skin.

Less is usually more. Most men prefer a natural look. On your next date, aim to be just a little more relaxed than you usually are about your hair, makeup and clothing. You'll be able to relax and enjoy his company, and you won't feel as if everything is riding on you looking your best. You'll move more elegantly if you feel comfortable. And, contrary to what your hairdresser might think, the less your hair resembles a mushroom the better.

Many years ago, a friend of a friend split up unexpectedly with his girlfriend, whom he'd been with for quite some time. He was quite funny and a very good son to his widowed mother. We had been acquaintances for a number of years, but I never felt fully relaxed in his company—not even with our mutual friend acting as a buffer. Our friend encouraged us to go out for a drink together. Neither of us was particularly attracted to the other, but a combination of boredom, desperation and curiosity had made us both a little more daring than usual. We finally agreed and forced ourselves, against our better judgment, to give it a go. We each knew the other person was not that keen, but neither of us wanted to be the one to admit it. As Camus said, the hardest thing to let go of is that which you don't really care for in the first place.

Every time I went on a date with him, I would spend a huge amount of money getting my hair and makeup done in a top salon beforehand, and he would show up having made minimal effort on his appearance. On our third date, he turned up looking even more unkempt than usual. I became really resentful. I'd invested so much money and time preparing for all our dates. Prior to any date, there is no need to do anything out of the ordinary. At most, you might book yourself in for a nice blow-dry in your local salon. Many men would be shocked by the price of a blow-dry, never mind a full-scale makeover. And any man worth your while would never expect you to go to such lengths to impress him.

Be True to Yourself

When you don't feel loved, it's easy to start to believe it's because you don't deserve love. You may feel insecure and inadequate, as though everything about you is wrong. In that case, it can be tempting to want to change yourself. Change is good; life is full of changes, and you are always growing. It's great to change the way you live and think and behave, but you don't need to change who you are inside.

Since you started reading this book, you've already made all kinds of positive changes in your life. You've begun to open up your attitude, vary your approaches, and break unhealthy patterns, which are all changes to the way that you move towards your goals and dreams. But you should never seek to change your core essence, because that's what makes you beautiful and special.

You don't have to change who you are in order to attract love. Being true to yourself makes you real. People can always sense what is real and they find it to be incredibly appealing. It's all about embracing your uniqueness, not emulating anyone else's. This chapter will show you different ways of exploring your individuality so that your true essence can shine. Once you connect with your true self, you'll learn that you deserve love and respect, and then others will want to love and respect you.

Fall in love with yourself

We all know someone who, despite being no more or less attractive than the rest of us, has men queuing up to ask her out. Instead of sitting around with your friends bitching about how she's not that hot, you might try to take on a bit of her attitude. She is the one to watch, as she effortlessly attracts men simply by being herself. What she has is far more powerful than a perfect smile, a rapier wit or an amazing career. There's just something about her that no one can quite put their finger on. Most likely, she grew up knowing that she was adored, but without having been spoilt or indulged. While it's certainly easier to love and accept yourself unconditionally throughout your life when your parents made you the centre of their universe since your early childhood, it's never too late to learn to love and value yourself. Why not start right now?

You may have heard people say of someone they regard as being annoyingly self-assured: *She's in love with herself.* Often when people say this, they are envious of the person's confidence. While it's intended as a putdown, it contains more than a grain of truth. It is about seeing yourself the same way a doting mother sees her child. There is no need to boast when you are already safe in the knowledge that your baby is the cutest one on the bus; you simply sit back and bask in the glow. To be true to who you are, you must start to regard the qualities you once considered ordinary or unattractive as endearing, captivating and unique. While it may take a while to fall in love with yourself, we know that all the best love stories start off slowly and end up somewhere quite unexpected.

If you can view yourself through loving and generous eyes, you'll truly like and accept yourself, and other people will sense it and be drawn to you. In this way you can be your own advocate. When a teacher sends their own child to the school where they work, whatever their true reasons may be for doing so, others will form the impression that they have faith in the school's academic standards and its ethos. Demonstrating your belief in yourself is a powerful way to prove your value.

You are faced with an exciting challenge. Take responsibility for creating your own happiness in the here and now. Start appreciating the woman that you have undervalued for all these years. Enjoying your own company will convey the message that you are an amazing person. Spend some quality time getting reacquainted with yourself, and enjoy it while it lasts, because before too long you will be in high demand. People are irresistibly drawn to those who exude self-acceptance.

Cultivate positivity, optimism and openness. We all know just how draining it can be to spend time in the company of someone who sees the negative in every situation, who is so discontented that they presume everyone else feels the same way. They are pessimistic about the future and resentful of other people's good fortune. They criticise any person or choice they don't understand. If you recognise any of these behaviours in yourself, I'd advise you to start spending time in the company of those who are open-minded and non-judgmental. Let their good attitude rub off on you. You will notice how much better you feel about yourself, your situation and others. People will be more eager to spend time in your company.

Select three role models. They may be friends, acquaintances or celebrities whose outlook you admire. Try to adopt the kind of attitude you think they would in your circumstances. My role models are three of my friends, whose upbeat, can-do attitude to life I deeply admire. I navigate awkward moments by trying to imagine how they would think, act or speak, and following suit. It has invariably worked for me, although I have had moments of weakness when provoked.

There are certain individuals whose company you can't avoid, but by changing how you see these encounters, you can change the nature of the exchange. In a radio interview with Wayne Dyer, a caller asked how to handle a relative who riled and irked her. Dyer advised the caller to regard this person as her greatest teacher. This woman's nemesis embodied an opportunity for growth. Our weakest points and biggest obstacles offer our souls an intensive workout and a chance to continue to evolve spiritually. Everyone contains so much innate goodness. By removing blocks such as negativity and criticism, we allow our truest and best selves to shine.

IGNORE ALL NEGATIVE INNER TALK!

Don't compare yourself to anyone else

The only competition you should ever enter into is one of authenticity, as you will always win first prize. People love spending time with those who are completely at ease with themselves. Complimenting other women on their looks, if done only to create the false impression that you are completely secure in yourself, will fool nobody, including yourself.

A friend of mine told me about one of her colleagues. This woman is attractive and has a wonderfully charismatic personality. She claims to see beauty everywhere and describes every girl she meets as being very pretty. She exchanges nods of approval with her male colleagues whenever an attractive woman joins their firm, in an effort to appear secure and cool to her male co-workers. Her female co-workers think otherwise. Whenever she has a few drinks on board, her insecurities surface.

She recently astounded all the guests at her wedding when she wrapped up her thank-you speech by saying that one of her bridesmaids had looked awful when they had been at college together, and that she was ever so grateful to have been on more than one occasion photographed next to her because it made her look so good by comparison. She was referring specifically to her bridesmaid's smile and skin, both of which had changed dramatically since their student days. Even though her friend now has straightened, whitened teeth and clear, glowing skin, she must have felt the sting of being reminded of what may have been an awkward time for her. The bride's comments were disrespectful to her friend, but she had demeaned herself most of all. How little must she have thought of herself to need to stand on someone else to make herself feel tall on her own wedding day!

On her special day, the bride outshines everyone. She needn't worry that her stunning sister or pretty best friend will steal the show. All eyes will be on her, resplendently amaranthine in her beauty. What if we applied the same principle in everyday life? It doesn't matter if half of the women on the high street are viewed as being conventionally better looking than you; if you act like the star of your own life, you will never have difficulty attracting men. Maybe not every man on the street will pursue you, but one very special man will be inexplicably drawn at a time when you are ready and searching for him. The only person you should ever try to be is yourself. You will always win, and it's a hell of a lot easier and infinitely more original than trying to be someone you're not. Oscar Wilde said it, and he knew a thing or two about being original.

DON'T GIVE UP! LET YOUR TRUE BEAUTY SHINE!

Resist the temptation to brag

This is one of the steps in the opening chapter, but it also applies to the topic of being true to yourself, and it's worth repeating. Sometimes, we are so damned chuffed with our lot in life that we'd like to let everyone know about it, usually because we don't fully believe we deserve it or that it will last. You must resist the need to boast. Ultimately, our aim in life is to gain others' affection and respect. Bragging distances us from the person with whom we are trying to connect, instead of bringing us closer to them, which is what we really want. The only type of praise that ever makes us feel good is the unsolicited kind, given by others. If you have any degree of self-awareness, you will feel your energy deplete and your mood darken after any attempt on your part to impress others. Self-praise is no praise at all, and it actually makes you feel a lot worse about yourself.

While your date may be awfully impressed by your PhD, your father's long and illustrious career on the bench of the High Court or the fact that you played badminton for your county as a toddler; he would be much more impressed if he were to find it out for himself. Talent and modesty are incredibly attractive to a potential partner. Truly brilliant and emotionally secure people have no need to advertise or namedrop. Although the temptation to sell yourself can be hard to resist, resist it you must. Just notice how you feel directly after you give in to the need to flatter yourself. It is not a good feeling and it is certainly not a good look! You will attract people who are needy or no one at all.

If you are sharing your news because you are overwhelmingly happy, and your intention is not to impress others but to let them know how blessed and grateful you feel, this will be obvious to all involved, yourself included. This does not qualify as boasting. You'll feel very differently after sharing in this way, more elevated than deflated. I briefly dated a man who tried to spin his unabashed boasting as an endearing quirk. He cultivated it to a rather annoying extent. He seemed to feel that it didn't count as boasting if he prefaced his story with a smirk and a reference to his dislike of false modesty. Humility means never having to say you're all that!

Don't settle for less than first place

This is not something you should be concerned with until you have been together for at least one year, as affection takes time to blossom and great loves are not grown overnight. You can't expect to be the love of his life straight off the bat, just as he can't expect to be yours. But if you've been together for at least one year, and you have good reason to believe you're not your partner's first choice, you should ask him about this as soon as possible.

Do not labour under the delusion that he is pining for someone else without ascertaining the facts. In Daphne du Maurier's gothic classic, *Rebecca*, the lead character completely misconstrues the nature of her husband's relationship with his first wife. What you perceive as an incredibly romantic story may appear that way because he's withholding the gory details. If it sounds like everything was perfect with his ex and he might be still madly in love with her, perhaps he's too much of a gentleman to air his dirty laundry.

He will likely clarify that you are indeed his most beloved. Even if at first he blunders through a response that you find unsatisfactory and unconvincing, this may be due to embarrassment more than anything else. If this is the case, he'll likely follow up with you afterwards and everything will be cleared up. If he doesn't tell you the truth, you'll know. In my experience, most people can't lie convincingly about these matters. Unless he looks directly into your eyes and proclaims that you are his first choice, move along and start looking for a man who will.

Many men (and some women) are more pragmatic than romantic. These people are quite comfortable marrying a person that they know full well is not the love of their lives. Do not settle for someone who is settling for you. Second place is a terrible place to start a lifelong partnership, especially if you are willing to put them first. Over the years, the disparity will erode the fabric of your relationship. In harder times, when stresses and strains are pulling you in different directions, do you really think he will keep coming back with any enthusiasm to someone who never quite lit up his world from the outset?

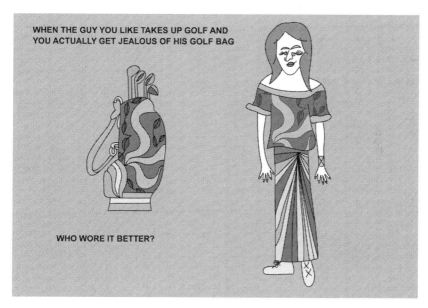

NEVER COMPETE FOR HIS ATTENTION! YOU ARE THE PRIZE!

AGAIN, YOU ARE PERFECT AS YOU ARE. NO NEED
TO CHANGE TO GAIN HIS ATTENTION!

DO NOT SETTLE FOR LESS THAN FIRST PLACE

Take a Leap of Faith

The objective of a conversation is to exchange views with the aim of learning something new, even if all you learn is that you still do not agree with the person you're conversing with on the question of God or any other topic. Attempting to make someone else bow to your superior knowledge and worldly wisdom is draining and ultimately futile. Allow others to think differently to you. You do not need someone else to validate your opinions or your worldview. People who proclaim to know that there is no God or other benevolent force guiding the Universe are just as entitled to their opinion as those of us who aren't sure. Trying to convince someone else of your strongly held beliefs leads nowhere. Nobody knows anything for sure, but everyone is entitled to believe. The arrogance of any person who tries to ram their views down other people's throats is more damaging than any view could be.

That said, I will make an argument of sorts for choosing to believe. Life is so much easier and holds more meaning when you trust that a benign force is working behind the scenes to ensure that justice will prevail. Faith guides your thoughts and actions in a positive way and enables you to play the long game, to stick with it, to try again, and to be resilient even when things are tough. Ultimately, you will be happier if you believe that everything is conspiring perfectly towards creating the greatest good. How you feel influences how you act; how you act shapes how you live; and how you live is your life!

Regard your lost opportunities in love and your romantic fails as practice runs for the real thing. You wouldn't wish to be tied up in a moderately satisfying relationship when the love of your life walks through the door. You are available, and it is simply a matter of time until your beloved appears in your life. Perhaps you are finding it rather difficult to muster the self-belief and blind faith required for this line of thinking. You can start by imagining how wonderful it would be if you unquestioningly believed in your ability to draw in love, regardless of your age, your life circumstances, your romantic history or any other factor which is believed to stand in the way of relationships.

Look at those individuals who say *when I get married* rather than *if I get married*. I used to perceive this as signifying arrogance, but now I see that it signals confidence and self-belief. They were speaking realistically about a future they utterly believed in. Just as cavemen drew pictures of the animals they planned to hunt, our intentions have the power to attract and govern outcomes. It doesn't come down to a question of luck, but expectation. When you believe good or bad will come to you, you draw it to you. When you expect happiness or sadness will be yours, you look for it and so that is what you'll find. That's why you'll often see wonderful and beautiful women repeatedly attracting the same type of unsuitable men or falling into one short-term relationship after another.

What you believe about yourself is so much more powerful than anyone else's view of you. There is no overarching objective reality anyway, so it is all a matter of perception and personal taste. If you believe that you deserve the love of a wonderful man, then that is what you will continually experience throughout your life. Begin to imagine what it would be like if you felt entitled to love. Watch those people in your life who have never had trouble finding love, particularly those who aren't possessed of stunning good looks. Would it be possible for you to believe in yourself as they believe in themselves? Accept that God or another benevolent force is working backstage at this very moment, and your ideal partner will step on stage when given his cue.

Why would humans have a spiritual element to their nature if there were no spiritual aspect to the Universe? Would we feel this undeniable pull to find out if there is more to this life than the material world, if there were nothing more? Since we will never know for certain either way, and because having faith has so many proven benefits, why not just believe?

No Pressure!

You may have decided that you must be in a steady relationship with long-term potential by the time you reach a certain age. You may have assigned that number to yourself or let friends, society or popular culture decide for you. Especially if you are nearing the deadline you have set for yourself, I'd advise you to push it back to a point in time called *when it's meant to be*.

Decisions made in haste and under pressure are often not propitious ones. If you're placing yourself under such enormous pressure, as many women do, you may start to feel desperate, making it only that much harder to be at your best and attract your perfect match. Although you may be tempted to blitz the dating websites and join every speed dating event in the run up to your self-assigned cut-off date, you must really take a step back and look at how crazy you are being. By dashing about desperately at the last minute, at best you may find a mildly suitable match or a moderately pleasing relationship, when you deserve so much more.

Years ago, I worked with a woman who was a few years older than me. She was extremely blessed in the looks department. She'd had a difficult childhood and spent two decades of her life dealing with undiagnosed severe obsessive-compulsive disorder. Her family had always joked about how fastidious she was about cleanliness, and they had somewhat encouraged and indulged her onerous rituals. Compulsive hand washing and checking, and a heightened aversion to germs, made socialising very difficult and rendered romantic relationships a landmine.

While in her late thirties, she'd received her diagnosis and had made great strides in dealing with her condition. Instead of enjoying her life for the first time in her adult life, she decided she had six months to find herself a husband and start a family. Although she managed to keep the germ phobia under wraps from most men in the early stages of dating, her pulsating anxiety to be in a relationship sabotaged her chances with any normal guy right from the outset. Having given up hope of securing a permanent job, she set her sights on marrying a well-paid professional and becoming a stay-at-home mum. The job market was pretty bleak at that time, so it wasn't an entirely crazy notion. The madness lay in her placing all these expectations on herself and on someone she hadn't yet met.

Just as women can detect even the faintest whiff of body odour, men have a way of sensing women with a plan. Had she relaxed her approach, let go of the notion of a sell-by date, and opened herself to the opportunity of meeting new and interesting men, one of them could have turned out to be the love of her life. But she was not in the habit of taking advice or letting life happen. She lived her life with an irrepressible urge to control external circumstances. She dated unsuitable men, scared all the regular guys away, and became increasingly anxious as her deadline approached. More than once, she rekindled a previously unsuccessful relationship with a past lover only to find herself unceremoniously dumped as soon as she broached the subject of marriage. At the time of writing, seven years later, she remains single. She has been through a lot, and I wish her great happiness in the future. I'm sure that if she can learn to be a little gentler with herself, things will work out beautifully for her.

Work at your own pace, trusting that the Universe will reveal your ideal man when both of you are ready. Relax, and remember to breathe. You are not a carton of milk; you do not have a sell-by date. Love is for people of all ages. Perhaps you are in a rush because you want to have children and would prefer to start at an earlier age. While it is true that fertility decreases as you get older, there are many options to assist you, and more women than ever before are giving birth in their forties. Your chances of meeting the right man greatly increase when you let go of your deadline, as you'll be more relaxed, which makes you infinitely more fun and attractive.

THERE IS NO UPPER AGE LIMIT WHEN
IT COMES TO FINDING LOVE!

Be Authentic

Some people advocate treating your potential suitor as your adversary: you must aim to trick, tease and fool him into falling more in love with you than he might otherwise. I feel it's much better to be honest and authentic. The type of man with whom you have to play games is not a genuine, open and kind-hearted one. Be yourself. By playing games and resorting to subterfuge, you would be sending a very clear and unequivocal message to him, and to yourself, that you're not likeable or lovable just as you are. This can serve only to make you feel anxious and needy. If someone doesn't think you're good enough for him, it does not mean you should try to hoodwink him into liking you. It means that he is clearly not discerning or discriminating in his tastes. The conclusion that you must draw from this is that he is not good enough for you.

As we discussed in Chapter One, your new type is Gilbert Blythe, the man who thinks you are stunning in your gym gear straight off the treadmill. Friends had told me over the years how meeting men in the gym or on the sports field was impossible. They felt you would have to be wearing a full face of makeup and flattering clothes if you wanted to be in with a chance of attracting a man. I don't believe this for a minute. If your eyes are bright, your skin is glowing, and your hair is smooth, as women often appear in the gym, then you are looking sufficiently fabulous to attract a man. Very few men go for the highly manicured look. You may be surprised to hear that men prefer women to wear minimal makeup and dress in a smart, casual manner. They are not half as keen on the overly processed Barbie-doll look as you might have been led to believe. And few things, if any, are more attractive than a genuine smile.

The Ripple Effect

There are days when you just feel that anything is possible. Maybe it's the change in the weather, the brighter mornings, the approaching holidays or simply a refreshing night's sleep. Who knows? But you feel the sense of possibility that permeated your younger years, before you became world-weary and despondent. You feel that things might just take a turn for the better. Try to recreate this feeling of hope, this sense of possibility, this inexplicable optimism and apparently unfounded excitement as often as you possibly can. In these moments, you bring yourself closer to realising your dreams.

By the time I embarked upon this process of finding love, I had become so negative and entrenched in pessimistic thinking that it was often hard for me to feel positive about relationships. Over the previous decade, too many things had happened. Or rather, they hadn't happened. The last drops of my youthful optimism had long since evaporated. I was bitter and fearful, convinced that I would never meet anyone. I felt as if I had been cursed, that I was destined to be eternally alone and lonely. My despondency was completely understandable; ten years is a long time to be sad and single, to receive little or no interest. It took some time to become hopeful again. Earlier, we discussed the power of meditation and affirmations. They really are powerful tools in transforming how you think and feel. If you can imagine how it would feel to be in a fulfilling relationship with an amazing man, you can simulate that feeling of quiet contentment or uncontainable joy, even if for only a minute or two. This will bring you closer to making real your long-held fantasy. Stop worrying about whether it seems realistic, and just feel it. All wonders and miracles seem unrealisable until they manifest. It seems unattainable—so what? Feel it anyway!

Look to other areas in which you have exceeded your own and other people's expectations. I now look to my relationship success to give me hope in my other pursuits. For most of my life, I had been single and lacked direction. This process helped me to change that. Sometimes when I feel that I will never taste success in another area of my life, I remind myself that I defied the bleak prognosis I'd given myself in the dating realm. If you have surprised yourself and achieved more than you expected in another area of life, use this as inspiration.

An acquaintance told me she hadn't spoken a word for the first few years of primary school. Apart from her sister, she had no friends until she started secondary school. There, she blossomed into a quietly confident and positive young woman who loved organising events. To this day, she is surprised to have been elected as one of the twelve prefects in her final year of school. Even in adulthood, she continues to question her worth. Acknowledging her success in one area of her life allows her to feel hopeful in others. When she despaired of ever finding a job, she looked to how she'd established herself as a well-liked and valued member of the school community. She found success in her career as a solicitor by getting excited about her new job before she'd even been called for an interview. Later, when she felt despondent about meeting a nice man, she looked to her other success stories. Success has a ripple effect. Rather than waiting to get excited, cultivate that feeling now, and you will speed up the arrival of your desired outcome.

WHEN YOU BELIEVE FOR A FULL FIVE MINUTES THAT YOU DESERVE THE LOVE OF A WONDERFUL MAN, YOU DRAW HIM THAT BIT CLOSER....

FROM HOPE TO FULL FAITH IS BUT A SKIP AND A JUMP

Nobody's Perfect

How you view someone's flaws is a good way to gauge how you feel about them. If you don't like a man all that much in the first place, you may view his shortcomings as a reason to stop seeing him altogether. If you already have a soft spot for him, you might happily overlook his dubious taste in shoes or his slight paunch.

The early days of a relationship can be dangerous territory that requires careful manoeuvring, as with the childhood game Operation. If the hook touches the wire, an electric buzz is generated, and you're out. The man may feel that he's walking on eggshells. He may, in his nervousness and eagerness to please, say and do things that are out of character for him. Or, you may notice something small that grates on your nerves a little. Given time, if you continue to focus on it, it may grow into an insurmountable obstacle. You may rule out a perfectly nice and eminently dateable man without justifiable cause.

Many women have a tendency to eliminate perfectly good men in the early stages of dating. If you are aware that you have this tendency, you might want to recalibrate your expectations. If you were a teacher who had set a test for a class, only to realise that it was pitched to students having higher proficiency or more experience, you would adjust your marking scheme accordingly. If you know you are prone to being overly critical, take a step back and question the snap judgments you might make about your potential partners.

Say you feel turned off by a man who is terribly nervous when speaking to you on the phone for the first time. Perhaps you were hoping he'd be the type of guy who is ultra-confident in every situation, no matter how daunting it may be. Instead of seeing his behaviour as a sign of weakness, you might take it as a compliment. This genuine and lovely guy is a little intimidated when speaking with you because he likes you so very much, and he doesn't feel the need to mask his nerves with machismo or bluster, because he's confident enough to reveal his real self.

This perspective paints both of you in a much more favourable light. It's not about being less judgmental, as much as it is about seeing the best in everyone and yourself in every situation, which will make you happier and more confident in the long run. See how much nicer it is to live your life as an accepting and kind person than as a hypercritical witch for whom nobody is ever good enough?

After I met Gilbert, we exchanged a few messages via Facebook over the Christmas period. Being in hypervigilant mode, I noticed a few errors in his grammar and spelling, and proceeded to ruminate on his eligibility as a partner. I mentioned my concerns to a friend, who felt I had every reason to be wary. She said that both she and her husband viewed bad grammar as a deal-breaker. I found their stance a little dramatic. Later that day, I discussed the matter with another friend. She wisely said that an excellent grasp of grammar was something to be required of a fellow member of one's book club or an academic collaborator rather than of a lover. A person's ability to diagram a sentence bears no relation to their ability to love you and care for you. This applies to many other bugbears as well. Your love for someone should not depend on their being perfect in every way.

DO NOT BREAK UP OVER A SPLIT INFINITIVE!

Why Do Relationships Happen to Bad People?

I recently ate at a lovely Japanese restaurant, where the sushi is superb and the hospitality unrivalled. Upon entering the restaurant, I couldn't help but notice a thirty-something woman scowling at the sight of my ten-month-old baby placidly sitting in his buggy. As I know my little boy behaves impeccably most of the time, I was not intimidated by her cold stare. She was dining with a fairly attractive man, and I listened in on their conversation. Eavesdropping is one of my favourite pastimes, and I was interested to see whether this woman would, in fact, turn out to have a pleasant character. She proceeded to criticise and deride a long list of friends, colleagues and acquaintances. She described one of them as being "only a teacher." I assumed that the poor bloke in her company must be her brother or related to her by blood. Who would sign up for a romantic relationship with such a spiteful creature?

Later, they strolled hand in hand out of the café. As he protectively ushered her across the road, I noticed a wedding ring glinting upon his finger. I was floored. *How is it possible that such an embittered woman is married while so many of my lovely friends remain single?* It didn't seem fair. Then I realised that I wouldn't wish her partner upon any of my friends, as he clearly has no need or desire for sunshine and brightness in his life. If he has chosen to be with a draining, negative partner, he must not be such a great catch either. As I watched them walk away, I pitied them. How boring it must be to listen to yourself or your partner constantly whine about how inadequate other people are! Back when I was single, I might very well have become frustrated if I had seen this nasty woman and her devoted husband. If I could speak to my former self, I would say, *Enjoy the run-up! A fun and positive relationship in which you both laugh and radiate joy is a million times better than a union mired in negativity.*

Is it my turn yet?

Do you ever feel as if the world has forgotten about you....

and you just want to check your number in the queue....

or if you're in the queue at all...............

IT WILL BE YOUR TIME SOONER THAN YOU THINK!

Green-Eyed Monsters

Everyone is susceptible to feeling jealous at times. It's perfectly normal. This emotion surfaces when we are feeling insecure or overwhelmed. It can drive us to engage in negative behaviour, such as questioning our partner's motives, tracking their every move or harbouring unfounded suspicions about them. Jealousy stems from a need for self-preservation. People may have hurt us in the past, and sometimes we respond by trying to prevent ourselves from being hurt again. By being hyper-vigilant to potential hurt or harm, we feel that we can somehow prevent ourselves from being betrayed again.

Sometimes jealousy gets out of hand. If you are feeling jealous, it makes you feel bad about yourself and your relationship. It's no fun being in a relationship with an overly jealous partner, either. It's hard to respect someone who is behaving in a possessive manner. If you are dealing with feelings of jealousy or a jealous partner, it is important to understand why someone becomes jealous in order to address the underlying issues. There is a school of thought that says the cure for jealousy is to starve your partner's insecurity by refusing to comfort them, withholding reassurance, and allowing them to feel their anxiety. I don't agree with this. Speaking as someone who suffered from crippling insecurity at the beginning of my relationship with the man I'm married to now, I would recommend reassuring your partner of your love for them and your loyalty to them. This will help them to feel safer in the context of your relationship.

If jealousy is the main theme of your relationship, then it is a serious problem that needs to be addressed in a professional setting with a qualified counsellor. If it is something you struggle with only occasionally and you are aware that your jealous behaviour, thoughts and feelings are unreasonable, and you are willing to work on them, a loving and caring partner may be able to help you through it. You need to make your partner aware of why you are feeling this way. Give him your back story, in order to help him see what circumstances have driven you to adopt this fearful response. Nobody is perfect; the more you get to know someone, the more you love their foibles and their idiosyncrasies.

A lovely and very attractive friend of mine started dating a man with whom she worked in a pharmacy. She told me that at the start of their relationship, she was so persecuted by intrusive thoughts that she often felt like ripping off her head and throwing it away. Even though he was entirely devoted and utterly loyal to her from the outset, she couldn't bear to see him talking to female customers, as she deeply feared that he would be attracted to them. As much as she hated being front of house, she would appear at the counter whenever a young, attractive woman entered the shop. She would insist on serving them, in order to limit his contact with them. Eventually, he noticed that something was up and broached the subject with her. She explained to him why she felt so insecure—all her previous boyfriends had been womanisers and her first husband had cheated on her with a co-worker. He reassured her in the most loving way possible that he had no interest in these women and that he had eyes only for her. They have now been happily married for ten years and have two delightful sons.

Living in a state of constant alert in order to prevent past hurts from reoccurring doesn't let you leave that pain behind, because you are choosing to live with the fear and the memory of that pain and to let it rule your life. The lengths to which you will be forced to go in order to protect yourself will drain all enjoyment from your life and threaten to sabotage your relationship. If you are harbouring residual insecurity from a previous relationship or life experience, make sure that you choose a partner who is understanding and non-judgmental. You will not match well with an intense man who is as prone to worry and over-analysis as you are. Choose someone who balances and calms you and is better at dealing with worry and stress than you are. He will make a much better life partner than someone who has the very same insecurities.

I briefly dated a man who was more insecure about his appearance than I was about mine. I spent the majority of our time together convincing him that we were suitably matched. I enjoyed the fact that, for once, I was the more secure person in the relationship, which probably made him feel even less secure. This was not a healthy basis for a relationship. The only way I could hold his attention was by making him jealous. There is no harm in a fleeting moment of jealousy if it serves to remind you of just how much you like someone. Beyond that, it will profoundly damage the relationship.

On Again, Off Again

On-again, off-again relationships can be dragged out for years or even decades. Ultimately, they go nowhere, and they drive you insane in the process. Being in such a relationship will frazzle your own head, as well as frying the brains and trying the patience of all your friends and family members. The drama of such relationships can very easily distract us from the truth of the matter; that there is no real depth to the bond. When we are completely consumed by the drama of passionate arguments and unexpected reunions, it is easy for us to overlook the fact that we don't have the same sense of humour, that he lacks compassion and depth of character, or any number of other deal-breakers.

Far too many women have wasted too many years trying to make a man into something he is not. It may be that his values are incompatible with yours or that he has a fear of commitment. Whatever his problem is with you, with himself or with the relationship, he is not the right person for you. You cannot untie another person's emotional knots. Once the pattern is established, there's no point in trying to make it work or hoping for a miraculous change. You had best let go sooner rather than later.

When such a cad senses that you are pulling away, he will very often present himself on a plate, with a big, juicy apple in his mouth. You may be surprised at how unappealing this offer seems when it unexpectedly and eventually materialises. As you develop greater respect for yourself by working on your self-esteem, you will find that you have less interest in him. As your affection for him begins to wane, a new man stands a very good chance of getting a foothold in your life, of making a positive impression and potentially becoming your future partner or husband.

A woman I know devoted twenty years of her life to a mirage. When she was in her late teens, she became involved with a man who had no interest in conducting a real relationship with her. After he moved abroad, they communicated primarily by texting. Meanwhile, she held down a decent job and enjoyed a full social life. They would spend time together whenever he returned to his hometown, which he did at least once a year. Every time she saw him, she would convince herself that he really meant it this time when he said he could see a future for them somewhere down the line. As she geared up for a long-distance relationship and started booking flights, her friends rolled their eyes and wondered when she'd learn. Once he was back in the UK, he would forget all about her and the false hope he'd given her. She was so madly in love with the idea of this man that she denied herself the chance to meet anyone else. She knew he wasn't committed to her, so she would date other men she met along the way, but as soon as it became serious, she would find some reason as to why it wouldn't work out with them.

After reaching the age of thirty-eight, she realised that she would have to get a move on if she ever wanted to start a family. After a long telephone discussion with her love interest, she decided to move to London. She tried to convince her friends and family that the distance between them had been the problem all along.

Without any hesitation about giving up her permanent job, she started applying for jobs in her field. When she secured an interview, she arranged to fly to London for the day. She asked if she could stay with him, but he told her he'd be out of the city on business. A few days later, she was offered the job. When she tried to call him with the good news, he was unavailable. She left him multiple voicemails, to which he finally responded with a text, asking if she was planning to accept the job offer. That's when the penny finally dropped.

It doesn't have to take this long for you to realise that someone is using you or stringing you along. Listen to your inner voice, your Higher Self, your instinct, or whatever you call it. It knows infinitely more than your conscious mind can ever know.

Me? Difficult?

I spent an afternoon listening to a woman list all the ways in which a man had offended her during the six months he'd been trying to date her. Professionally, this woman is at the top of her game. She's an architect with a successful practice, and her relationships with her clients are based on mutual respect and genuine fondness. However, a very troubled early life has predisposed her to anger and aggression. She told me that this man had invited her to a Christmas drinks party at his parents' house one Saturday night in early December. She neither attended the party nor acknowledged his calls or texts following up on the invitation, as she thought it quite impertinent of him to presume that she would appreciate such an offer. To this day, I don't understand what exactly she found so offensive about his invitation.

On the other hand, she did not seem to object to the frankly dangerous and harmful behaviour he admitted to engaging in while inebriated. For example, he had broken into a friend's house to steal a wad of cash he knew his friend intended to spend on a mutual friend's twenty-first birthday present. On another occasion, he had taken money from the bedside locker of his sleeping housemate and insinuated that another housemate might have taken it. She seemed to find this behaviour attractive. This is an

example of someone who has difficulty setting appropriate boundaries in her personal life.

There comes a certain point where we need to stand back and
take responsibility for our actions in the here and now. She has a
reputation for pushing friends' buttons—she suggested I get breast
implants to improve my success with men, for example. But while
we have all survived the jibes and cutting putdowns, she continues
to suffer, having isolated herself from loved ones and potential
partners. The person she's hurting the most is herself. Be aware
of toxic patterns in your friendships and relationships. Be willing to engage in open discussion with a neutral party, such as a
counsellor, if you feel that you may be sabotaging your chances at
happiness. If you find fault with every person in your life, it might
be time to consider that other people are not the problem, after all.

Power Games

At dinner one Valentine's Day, I sat next to a couple who never stopped competing with each other; each of them wanted to be regarded as the more desirable and more in demand of the two. When they spotted a girl they both knew at the other end of the restaurant, they proceeded to discuss her at great length for a large portion of the evening. The man admitted to liking her when he was younger. All of his anecdotes were littered with insinuations that this woman was far more attractive than his current girlfriend, who was sitting opposite him. In her own stories she portrayed herself as a femme fatale, who was being pursued by every man in town. Although they each experienced fleeting moments of victory, at the end of the night when they left the dining room, they must have felt simultaneously deflated and on edge.

It seemed to me that the man was well aware that his date was considerably more attractive than him. Instead of being delighted by his good fortune, he spent the entire evening trying to tear her down. Perhaps this was his way of restoring equilibrium to what he perceived to be an unbalanced match. The girl, feeling hurt and angry, tried to assert herself by putting down the other girl and boasting about her own appeal. Both parties were acting out of insecurity; neither party was showing affection or concern for the other. They both must have felt even less secure after the tense and disconnected exchange. The more time they spent in each other's company, the further apart they seemed to grow.

If, for whatever reason, you do not want the best for your partner, or if he resents your success or is intimidated by it, then you don't belong together. Some people who are capable of great kindness towards and affection for one partner are, for any number of reasons, a destructive force in another person's life.

You and your partner should want the very best for each other. If you do not, you must examine your motives. It's time to learn to understand yourself a bit better or to seek out another partnership altogether—one in which you collaborate and support one another instead of being locked in competition.

Serial First-Daters

A few years ago, I found myself talking to a friend of a friend at a barbeque. She was an avid proponent of online dating and had even managed to convince her father of its merits. He had also started dating online. She couldn't sing its praises highly enough. She assured me that it really did work—she had been going on at least one date per weekend for the last two years. The dates were always first dates, they never led to second ones. She was what I call a serial first-dater.

I was gobsmacked by her endorsement of this type of dating. I am all for Internet dating, if it works for you. I have a number of friends who went on to marry the first man they connected with via a matchmaking website. But if this girl was looking for more than a string of first dates, as I imagine she was, then this approach was not working for her. Hope springs eternal and all that, but most people would be truly exasperated and disillusioned after such an experience, rather than feeling pumped up and eager to recruit new enthusiasts.

Beware of the serial first-dater. While most women would be tearing their hair out after even a few months of such fruitless dating, there are a fair few men out there who actually enjoy repeating the first-date experience on a loop for the rest of their lives. About fifteen years ago, I went speed dating with a large group of friends. One girl connected with a guy who has a PhD in biology. I don't know why he felt the need to share that piece of information in the two minutes he spent talking with her, but she was sufficiently impressed to agree to a future date in another setting. He turned out not to be her type. A few years later, when I ventured back onto the speed dating scene, I encountered him once again. During our very brief encounter that night, he managed to shoehorn into our very brief chat the fact that he had a PhD. It appears that he had never left the speed dating scene and continued to mindlessly pursue the same goal using the same tactics week after week, year after year.

While it's admirable to remain hopeful in the face of defeat, the fact that he would have the same two-minute conversation with a different woman several years later shows a lack of variety in his approach. Don't get involved with a man who does not respond to your conversational cues about who you are or what you are interested in. He does not see or value what makes you unique, as he is looking for a woman—*any* woman. Such men don't see women as individuals in our own right or as their equals, and as such, they often emerge as womanisers. You can trust your instincts on this one.

Begrudgers

If anybody in your life is not sufficiently impressed by your fine qualities to throw a compliment your way at least every once in a while, get rid of them. There is nothing worse than a begrudger. Because a begrudger does not think highly of themselves, they fear that acknowledging your strengths or achievements will reveal their inferiority. Some people deal with low self-esteem by turning it in on themselves; others project it outwards and punish anyone who they feel is better than they are. They may have a lot going for them, but because they doubt their intrinsic value, they cannot see their potential. They want you to feel just as badly as they do. It's nothing personal against you; it's all about them. They will try to bring you down with backhanded compliments or petty slights, and by withholding praise.

No man is an island; everyone needs a little encouragement at times. We all have times when we agonise over our perceived inadequacies. Some of us are never quite sure whether we are considered attractive or plain; we may feel lovely one day and hideous the next. Some of us are self-conscious about our qualifications (or lack thereof), our personality, our accent or myriad other things.

It is not unreasonable to expect your partner to build you up when you're feeling low or to encourage you when your self-belief is waning. No one should make you feel needy for wanting reassurance and support through difficult times or a heartfelt compliment to lift you up once in a while.

We all know which friends and family members will build us up and which ones will tear us down. Yet we may continue to seek validation from people who have shown us, time and time again, that they are in the habit of withholding praise and approval, and that they might even take pleasure in stoking our insecurities. The reason this habit is so hard to break is that we don't believe we deserve better. It's as if we are daring them to confirm our worst fears. We have to let go of this self-destructive impulse in order to break the cycle.

I recently sought reassurance from someone I have known for years. Instead of supporting me, she further damaged my self-esteem, which was already in a fragile state. Worst of all, she clearly took pleasure in my pain. If she were a colleague or a neighbour, I would have known by now that she is not the type of person you go to when you need a boost. As much as it hurt to be reminded of how inadequate she thinks I am, what hurt even more was realizing that, once again, I chose to put myself in a vulnerable position with someone who does not have my best interests at heart. This is a life lesson I am still trying to learn. Some people will hurt you. Do not give your heart to people who will only trample over your feelings.

SURROUND YOURSELF WITH POSITIVE PEOPLE
WHO ENCOURAGE AND BELIEVE IN YOU

What Does Your T-Shirt Say?

Although we may believe ourselves to be emotionally complex and sophisticated, we are simple and predictable creatures. Our friends and family know (often better than we know ourselves) how we might react to a given situation, outcome or comment. We each have our bugbears and bandwagons. Certain subjects aggravate us to the point of distraction or even destruction. A situation or topic that inflames us will not have the same effect on a person with a different life history and experience.

My hairdresser once asked me why it was that people were always insulting me. It gave me pause for thought. What was I doing or saying to other people to elicit their criticism? It made me question whether I might be inviting negative input or taking other people's opinions far too personally. If you hand someone a loaded gun, you can't be surprised if they shoot you. At times when I felt insecure and unable to trust my own judgment, I asked other people for feedback, on my appearance, in particular. Instead, I should have been asking myself why someone else's opinion of me mattered more to me than my own.

I had been running around looking for validation, approval and praise from all and sundry. I must have sounded like a broken record. I might as well have been wearing a T-shirt that said IRATE THAT OTHERS DON'T SEE MY VALUE. I made a conscious decision to start working on my catchphrase. Real change is gradual, so it wouldn't have been realistic to make the leap straight to LOVING AND ACCEPTING MYSELF TODAY AND EVERY DAY, REGARDLESS OF ANYONE ELSE'S OPINION; I did it in increments, like upgrading a car or a phone. I started with IRATE THAT I DON'T SEE MY OWN VALUE. Once I grew into that slogan, I upgraded to a more emotionally sophisticated one that embraced greater happiness and freedom, and it continues to grow with me.

In practical terms, the first step was to stop asking the negative people in my life for feedback on my appearance. I had spent the previous thirty years asking other people how I looked. Breaking that habit was hard, as I remained single and had yet to feel truly desired by anyone. But now, whenever I succumbed to my need to seek approval from people with a proven tendency to disappoint me, I knew I was responsible for my pain.

A year or so after I stopped seeking validation from those people, I started to have more faith in my own judgment. I found myself in situations in which I really wanted to check with others about what they thought of my new hair colour, shade of foundation or lip liner, but I was able to resist the urge. As my trust in myself grew, I saw myself as a more attractive person. Eventually, I reached a place where I liked myself regardless of what other people thought—or what I thought they thought. This is an ongoing struggle for me, but it is a battle I am fighting and will continue to fight. My T-shirt now says I FEEL MORE ATTRACTIVE EVERY DAY. I composed the following affirmation for times when I feel the need to seek approval.

I look in the mirror,

I like what I see,

I trust in my own opinion of me.

Stop Whining

I love hearing interesting life stories and am prepared to empathise with anyone—friend or stranger—who has been disrespected and abused.

But some people are perpetually hard done by and they never stop talking about it. You know someone like this: her family mistreats her; her boss misunderstands her; she has been given the runaround by some awful men and been terminally overlooked by some average ones.

We have all known this person; at times, we may have been this person. If your primary mode of conversation consists of sharing your grievances, you probably have begun to find it tiresome. Just imagine how exhausted your friends are. You may have lost one or two along the way. There comes a point when you have to zip it and get on with your life. Only when you become the friend on the receiving end of all that angst, anger, victimhood and regret do you realise how much of a drag you must have been.

Conversations should be a two-way street, not a dumping ground for one emotionally fragile and unfulfilled friend. Having a direct line to someone else's misery 24-7 is not a friendship; that type of relationship has entered into the domain of therapy. Occasionally airing your grievances is cathartic and allows your friendship to grow and deepen, but any more than that is destructive for both parties and to the friendship.

In my youth, I took for granted a kind friend who had lent me a listening ear on a few occasions. Because she showed such compassion the first time that I had broached a particular subject, I presumed she would always be willing to listen to my woes, regardless of what was going on in her own life. I cringe now when I think back to how I bombarded her with messages and calls, never thinking to ask what was going on with her.

If you want to attract into your life a positive, healthy man, whose main role is not merely to validate you in your misery and reinforce your role as victim, you have to be equally emotionally stable and well-balanced. When your need for pity outweighs your need for respect, and when a friend's sympathy, support and reassurance are the main currency of your relationship, you leave no room for laughter, learning or growth. A mutually beneficial friendship, in which you both share your stories and reflect on how you have been changed by your experiences, contains love and support for you both. If you are always complaining, you'll exude dissatisfaction and negativity, and positive people will not be drawn to you. It will be that much harder to attract someone into your life who will encourage you to grow and change for the better.

This is not to say that friendship should only be about the good times. No true friendship was ever forged out of good times alone. Without pain and conflict, we and our friendships would lack depth. But if friends are avoiding you or not returning your calls, ask yourself whether you are giving your issues a disproportionate amount of airtime. Ask yourself if you are leaching all the colour and joy from your friendships. If the answer is yes, then you have no choice but to quit complaining and to shift the focus to those around you.

If you have only bad news to report, and you feel that everyone else is so much better off than you are, why not change the topic of conversation to some of that goodness that is going around? Give it a rest and ask your friends how they're doing. Let them speak about what's good in their lives. Celebrate their successes, and let their good fortune reflect some light and positivity into your life.

Stop and Smell the Roses

As lonely as your present situation may feel at times, you will one day come to miss certain aspects of it. The single life contains many small luxuries that we fail to appreciate because we are so focused on what we desire. Even though you'll gladly trade these luxuries for a happy future with your ideal partner when the time comes, why not enjoy them while they last? You will never sleep as soundly as you do now; you will miss being able to stretch out across the full breadth of your double bed or flick on the light and read a few pages of a book if you happen to wake up in the middle of the night. In the early days of the relationship, you will be consumed with waiting for and obsessing over text messages and phone calls to such an extent that you may begin to wonder whether it's all worth it. It is.

Savour the parts of your life that please you now. If you are planning to have children, be warned that sleep, independence and freedom will be in short supply for a few years. Make the most of those pleasures while they are in abundance. Don't squander them by waiting around and focusing on what you lack. You've accepted that your ideal partner is on his way to you. Now you have the chance to find out who you are and how you love to live before someone else comes into your life with their own tastes and demands, and turns it upside down. Treasure these days.

When I was learning to embrace what was special about the life that I was making for myself, I rekindled my love affair with literature and cinema, and I relished the freedom and independence of owning my own apartment and having the time and money to go on spiritual retreats. I learned to appreciate my positive mental attitude, which had helped to sustain me through a decade of abject loneliness. I began to see that I had done incredibly well, given the circumstances. When you start to appreciate the beauty in yourself and your life, you'll be happier and have more fun, and time will move faster. Before you know it, love will manifest.

Stop Trying to Be So Cool

We all have been in situations where we're tempted to lose our cool: your boyfriend calls you by his ex's name, cancels his plans with you at the last minute or ogles another woman right in front of you. You want to blow a gasket, but you don't want to come across as crazy and overemotional, so you play it cool. You feel that because he wouldn't flip out over something small like that, neither should you. You rationalise his behaviour and swallow your emotions.

Guess what? You don't have to do that. It's a mistake to override or mask your emotions in order to try to replicate his behaviour. The two of you are wired differently, and he knows that. He will sense your discomfort, or your emotions will rise to the surface at a later point. Either way, he will know that you have been less than genuine. This is not to say that you should huff and puff whenever things upset you, but that you should value yourself enough to firmly stand your ground. If something he does upsets you, let him know. Be honest about how it makes you feel. If he's a good guy, he will appreciate the input and strive to do better. And he'll respect you much more for being real with him.

Men like cool women. They love hanging out with these women but don't necessarily fall in love with them. Although many men say they want to be with an easy-going, laid-back woman, when they actually meet a woman like this, they are likely to dismiss her as a potential partner. Instead, they will view her as they do their male friends. I've noticed that really cool women—the ones who act like men—often remain single. That is, until they meet that special guy who makes them feel a little crazy and a lot less cool.

You might wish you were not the kind of person who takes things personally, but some things should be taken personally. If he does something that crosses your limits, you have to trust that you have set those limits appropriately and value yourself enough to express your honest reaction. There is nothing wrong with being a little unreasonable every once in a while.

Some men are incredibly insensitive. They seem to make one grossly inappropriate remark after another. Others may test your boundaries by turning up late or cancelling a date at the last minute. These men are, consciously or unconsciously, attempting to gauge just how much they'll be able to get away with further down the line. A person is usually on their best behaviour in the early stages of a relationship. If he is already showing you a lack of respect, this is a red flag. Clearly communicate your expectations, and he will either rise to meet them or fall short. Being authentic and true to yourself is essential at any stage of a relationship, because it sets a precedent that you have boundaries which you are prepared to enforce. At the same time, do not be ruled by fear. You can stand your ground while remaining somewhat flexible and open. Both of you should allow the other person some leeway and the opportunity to learn from their mistakes.

DO NOT TOLERATE SHODDY BEHAVIOUR,
YOU DESERVE MUCH MORE!

Keep On Keeping On

At some point, you may feel like giving up. Allow yourself some time out. Spending a day wallowing in self-pity will not undo the progress you have made. Sometimes taking a few steps back will help you to gain the momentum to take the next forward leaps and bounds. Don't berate yourself for having a bad day. You don't have to force yourself to think positively about something that feels really hopeless at that particular point in time. Check in with that negative thought or emotion, discard it, and then distract yourself by doing something you enjoy.

No stance is final—you're allowed to change your mind. Go ahead and shake your proverbial fist at the entire male population for a day or two; it will feel good and won't significantly slow your progress along the path toward true love. When you do come across a lovely man a few days later, you'll appreciate him all the more. If this man happens not to be single, don't feel discouraged. View him as evidence that fine men do exist. Celebrate this fact and know that your ideal man is making his way towards you.

In the distant past, each time I met a nice man who was already in a relationship, I felt disheartened. It served only to confirm my fear that all the good ones were taken. Soon after I embarked upon my journey of positive expectation, I began to view happy couples as evidence of what also was possible for me. Whenever I saw a lovely couple walk down the street hand in hand, radiating happiness and warmth, I felt joy. While still single, I attended a party with four delightful couples, each comprising partners who were very different yet perfectly matched. I remember feeling so hopeful; the very sight of them instilled in me a confidence that my turn would come.

STAY POSITIVE WHEN YOU FEEL LIKE
GIVING UP! HE IS ON HIS WAY!

See Potential Everywhere

When I was single, I often wondered: *What's the best possible mindset for finding love?* Many people told me to relax, it would happen when I least expected it. Others encouraged me to be proactive: I should be getting out there and participating in as many singles events as I possibly could. How might I integrate these two wildly different approaches? I feared that I might jinx my chances by focusing too much on it—a watched pot never boils!

I had incorporated meditation, visualisation and affirmations into my daily routine. Most importantly, I had accepted that meeting a wonderful man was possible. At times, I felt that it was probable. I tried not to focus on any particular man or type of man; I cultivated the feeling of being completely relaxed and comfortable in the presence of someone who made me feel special. To be honest, I did not feel optimistic all or even most of the time. But I felt sufficiently excited and expectant for long enough each day to draw in my soul mate. I did not plan to ask anyone to set me up on a blind date. In the moment, I seized the opportunity to ask an old school friend to set me up with one of her husband's friends. On my first few dates with Gilbert, I did not expect that we would fall in love and get married. It slowly dawned on me that he was the only man for me.

Do not become too attached to highly specific outcomes. Having narrow expectations about what he will look like or where you'll meet him renders you less open to possibilities. See potential everywhere you go. Cultivate an attitude of excitement and anticipation along with an open mind. Accept in your heart that love is rightfully yours and release the need to control outcomes. This delightfully relaxed attitude of acceptance will make you more attractive to that man who has already started his journey towards you.

Your Type

In my experience, women love to talk about their type. Have you ever noticed how it's always tall, dark and handsome? No one ever describes their type as being short, pale with a characterful face, though many highly attractive men fit the latter description. I have heard many women say about their partners: *Even though I adore him, he is not my type.* Often, these women have an inflated sense of their own attractiveness. They hope their listener will be shocked and heartened to learn that they have mustered feelings of love for someone who doesn't meet their standards. In fact, they are revealing their own shortcomings, in failing to see what's truly attractive about their partners and in feeling entitled to announce this to the whole world.

Too much focus on appearance, whether it's your own or that of others, will lead you down the wrong path. What matters most is a man's character. Instead of defining your physical type, think about the characteristic traits and strengths you value in a person: honesty, kindness, loyalty, adaptability. A sense of humour doesn't hurt. In the first chapter, I introduced you to Gilbert Blythe. This is the type of man who deserves your attention and appreciation.

By the same token, you should not obsess unnecessarily over your own appearance. Although you may not be every man's type, there is without a doubt a man out there for whom your beauty shines. Assigning yourself, or anyone, male or female, a number out of ten is degrading to everyone. You are a unique individual. Nobody's true beauty, the inner or the outer kind, can equate to a number. Open your eyes to all the men out there who are wishing for someone as unique as you.

YOU ARE NOT A NUMBER!

BEWARE – PEOPLE WHO ARE MEAN WITH THEIR MONEY
ARE MEAN WITH THEIR TIME AND THEIR PRAISE TOO.

Dropping Hints

Back when we first started dating, Gilbert often would not call me for a day or two, especially when he was away on a golf trip. As a result, I would start to fret about his level of interest in me. Looking back, I can see that I needn't have worried, but at the time I was highly anxious about our relationship. Ideally, I wanted him to call me at least once a day. Once he got up to speed with this, I increased my requirement to two calls a day. I knew this stemmed from my insecurity rather than from a genuine desire to stay in regular contact.

Still, there were days when he forgot to call. One Sunday night, we watched a soap opera together on TV. In one scene, a female character stormed off in a dramatic fashion, and the male character with whom she had been talking was left nonplussed. Gilbert asked me if I had been following the series and whether I knew what this particular character had done to irk her so. I saw an opening to drop a not-so-subtle hint about what had been playing on my mind. I said that perhaps the male character had been away for the weekend playing golf with his friends and hadn't bothered to call her. He laughed. I laughed. Message received—or so I presumed. I gave myself a little pat on the back for having so deftly gotten my point across.

A few weeks later, he let a day pass without calling me. I was at a loss as to how this could have happened. I couldn't have made myself any clearer, could I? As it turns out, I could have. When I reminded him of my joke and how he had knowingly laughed, he said he had no memory of this conversation and informed me that he wouldn't have gotten the hint anyway.

It is always better to be clear and direct with your partner. Don't expect him to read your mind or parse your every statement for clues about your needs and desires. Most men simply do not operate this way—they assume that if there is a problem, you will let them know. State in a pleasant tone what you'd like him to do differently and why you would prefer him to do it this way. Provide examples and elicit his input. Let him know that you understand the logic and intentions underlying his actions and encourage him to suggest other ways he might have behaved. Open up a dialogue rather than telling him off and he will be more likely to act differently in the future.

Heart to Heart

Many people believe it is best to limit conversation to the realm of small talk during the first few dates. For fear of over-sharing or revealing their shortcomings, many daters stick to tried and tested topics: work, hobbies, number of siblings, and so on. But have you ever really hit it off with your female friends as a result of a bland conversation about neutral topics like the weather or your holiday plans?

When you converse about a topic that interests or excites you, whether it be a cringeworthy character on a reality TV programme, the key suspect in an ongoing court case or the neighbour who cut you off in the car park, you find out whether your conversational partner is your type of person. Do they share a similar sense of irony, outlook or life experience? Small talk doesn't allow us to get close enough to another person to find out who they truly are. Widening the range of topics increases the potential to make a connection. That is not to say that you will increase your chances of hitting it off with this person, but you will find out a lot more quickly whether or not you gel with them. How you appraise this comes down to instinct.

Move away from bland topics such as how you take your coffee. Some people see this as an opportunity to flirt with their date.

I don't take sugar in my tea, I'm sweet enough already. Ick. Strive to have a meaningful conversation in which you might actually learn something about each other. If you like what you hear or the way they tell a story, you have learnt that this is someone you might enjoy spending time with and may even grow to like. You are more likely to go on a second date if you can recall that funny or fascinating thing he said.

I remember Gilbert telling me about a friend of his who had shared a bedroom with his brother when they were growing up. I can't remember exactly how this was relevant to his anecdote, but I remember that I must have seemed surprised, because he went on to say that sharing bedrooms was indeed something people did in the countryside. It made me laugh and endeared him to me each time I recalled that evening in the days that followed.

Ex Maniacs

I was friends with an ex maniac. Whenever he had a few too many drinks on board, he would tell the tale of The One Who Got Away. Every time the topic of relationships came up, he would tell me and our friends about how he and his ex-girlfriend hadn't been able to make it work because the two of them were just too different. Her childhood sweetheart had broken her heart, and she had never fully recovered from it. He was terrified of hurting her, or so he said. Even though their story sounded like an ordinary tale of incompatibility, he revelled in its sadness.

The first time he told the story, I believed it. But with each repetition, more holes appeared. As much as he claimed to have liked her, he spoke of her in a disparaging way that did her no favours. She had no sense of style. She was socially awkward with his college friends, having never been to college herself. She hated reading and preferred to watch reality TV. What's more, when she spent a year working in London, he never visited her once. We were meant to believe that this was his great love. All I took from his stories was that he was a very bad boyfriend. At that time in her life, she didn't have much self-confidence, and his messing her around further eroded what little she had. The more he spoke of his heartbreak and lost love, the less I believed him.

As some of the women in our group were newly single, I began to wonder if he told this story in the hopes of appearing more attractive to them. Perhaps he just loved the attention. It seems he was incapable of severing ties, not only with his ex but with the story to which he had grown so attached. It was like The Bridges of Madison County, but without the sexual chemistry or the physical attraction. He might have used his time more productively by putting pen to paper and writing a novel or screenplay.

Ex maniacs are to be avoided at all costs. They bear unhealthy attachments to unhealthy relationships. A relationship can move forward only when neither party remains emotionally invested in a relationship or a person from the past. Being emotionally available means living in the present and looking to the future. It means having all of your energy and enthusiasm free and available to invest in the current relationship. If he brings up his ex on the first date, run for the hills.

Loose Lips Sink Friendships

When you see a friend engaging in behaviour that you believe to be damaging to their relationship, you may feel compelled to tell them so. This rarely, if ever, has a positive outcome. If you feel that your friendship with this person may not withstand your interference, you may be tempted to discuss their relationship with others who may or may not know them.

If you're talking about someone, and it is not with a view to helping them, you're gossiping. This is disrespectful to your friend and their partner. Bad news travels fast, so any rumours you spread will circle back to your friend. You risk damaging her relationship and destroying your friendship. Every pair has their own quirks and special ways of relating to each other, and you can't presume to understand them. You are not in a position to pass judgment on other people's relationships. Nor does it reflect positively on you when you feel entitled to put others down.

Many years ago, an acquaintance told me with a certain amount of satisfaction that both of her brothers' marriages and her daughter's marriage were on the brink of divorce. But to the best of my knowledge, all three of these relationships remain strong today. We have a tendency to look outwards at times when introspection and self-reflection are most needed in our own lives and relationships.

When we find ourselves compelled to scrutinise or criticise other people's relationships, we might first ask ourselves whether we are projecting onto their relationships doubts or discontent from within our own. If I hear someone talking about how a friend of theirs is going to boot out their husband at the earliest opportunity, I take it with a grain of salt, while also wishing the best for the couple. As for the person who is speculating, I also wish them the best in their relationship.

Safety First

Some people are reluctant to try online dating, because they feel it's too risky. They say: *You don't know who's out there!* While that is certainly true, I feel that life is too short to avoid situations that could bring your soul mate to you. Just make sure to exercise caution, just as you would when meeting anyone for the first time.

Years ago, I met someone online whose profile seemed dubious. He claimed to have a PhD in business, despite having no interest in books or reading. He didn't have a photo available for other members to view and sent me a photo he'd taken of what appeared to be someone else's photo in a magazine. Nothing about this guy or his profile seemed real.

When he suggested that we meet for the first time at a motorway exit, I declined but didn't immediately block him. A friend had been encouraging me to give anyone and everyone a chance, so I tried to give this guy the benefit of the doubt, even though we had barely communicated via the site. He then suggested meeting near my apartment, so I told him what neighbourhood I lived in. He said he didn't want to pay for parking and asked me to meet him in a suburb on the other side of the city. Having regularly worked there, he knew parking was free. I listened to my gut. I knew this chap was either very weird, very mean or very psychotic, and I didn't care to find out exactly which of these it was. I deleted his number. A few weeks later, he sent me a sexually explicit text. Fortunately, all contact ceased after that.

Sometimes I wonder what would have happened had I agreed to meet him. If someone you encounter online suggests meeting in a remote location, block him, and report him to the website administrator. If you ever feel that something is not quite right about the man with whom you are corresponding, pay close attention to that feeling. If it persists, walk away. It's always best to err on the side of caution.

Trust your gut. Let a friend know where you are going. Only agree to meet in a public place such as a restaurant. Let the man know that you have shared with someone else the details of your date. You can ask a friend to call you halfway through the date to check up on you. All moral judgments aside, it's best not to go back to his place at the end of the first date, as you cannot know with any certainty whether or not he is sane. This is purely about keeping you safe.

On Insecurity

Even after doing all this work on myself, I still have days when I feel unattractive, unconfident and unsuccessful, as will you. We are human, after all. I take comfort in the fact that even the greatest and most gifted of people doubt their worth and talent. I am no longer surprised when I hear an intellectually curious, engaging friend of mine wonder whether she should have more friends. That's a human tendency. Think about your circle of friends; most people expend an inordinate amount of energy agonising about an aspect of themselves that is, in fact, their best feature or trait. Charles Bukowski hit the nail on the head when he wrote:

> *"The problem with the world is that the intelligent people are full of doubts, while the stupid ones are full of confidence."*

Keep your chin up! Chances are, while you're obsessing over your imagined flaws, others are marvelling at your failure to recognise how wonderful you really are, how blind you are to your own brilliance.

On Integrity

Your relationship with yourself is always in flux. Your self-image may fluctuate dramatically even within a short period of time. You may feel that you are eminently likeable and socially adept one minute and hopelessly awkward the next. How we act greatly influences how we view ourselves. While stalking your boyfriend's exes on social media, you cannot possibly feel cool and confident. When speaking badly of others in an attempt to feel better about yourself, you will invariably feel worse. When you behave without integrity, you will find it difficult to truly like and respect yourself.

Act like the person you want to be. There is nothing insincere, disingenuous or fake about wanting to be a better person, a kinder friend, a more loyal sister or a more secure and accepting girl-friend. It doesn't mean you're trying to be something that you're not; you're simply mitigating the impulse we all have to tear down others when we are not feeling so great ourselves. While it's easy to feel magnanimous when everything is going your way, you must strive to keep your balance when things are not. The best way to keep your self-image in check is to always strive to behave in a manner consistent with your core values. And if you happen to have a single friend or colleague who is struggling to find love, don't just empathise, set her up!

GO ON, SET HER UP!

Once Upon A Time

Some time ago, a friend of a friend announced her imminent marriage to a man she had met only six months prior. I found myself wishing that the story of how I had met my husband was somehow different—more dramatic or romantic, perhaps. With us, it wasn't love at first sight. It didn't dawn on me until after our second date that he was someone really special. Our third date confirmed my hopes that he was someone worth getting to know. One hour into our fourth date, the best I'd ever had, I knew I would not be pursuing my plan to take a sabbatical the following year to work in Canada. Our relationship developed organically. As the months passed, we fell deeper and deeper in love. I could not believe my luck—I still can't, really.

Every couple has their own story of how they met and how their love grew. While your friend's romance may have blossomed at the speed of light or your co-worker may have received a marriage proposal on the fifth date, those are their stories. Let other people have their fireworks and whirlwinds. Swoon all you want, and rejoice on their behalf, but there's no need to envy them. Your love story will be perfectly unique to you and your partner. It will happen exactly as it should, and you wouldn't want it any other way.

Dating Dilemmas

I'd like to share with you some of the dating and relationship dilemmas that my friends and I have faced and discussed over the years, along with the advice I wish I could have given myself or my friends if I had known then what I know now.

A guy at my new place of work seemed interested in me at first, but lately he hasn't made any moves in my direction and seems indifferent at times.

How does he behave socially towards other people? If he's fairly confident and outgoing, and he hasn't approached you, this means he isn't interested in you. You may have misread his signals; perhaps he was simply being friendly. Save yourself a lot of angst and anxiety by letting go. On the other hand, if he seems socially inhibited, then he may be interested in you but simply too shy to approach you. You can always strike up a friendly conversation and give him the opportunity to move things to the next level. If he fails to do so during your first or second conversation, you need to move on. If he does eventually pluck up the courage, he knows where to find you. You should not be required to do all the work. If you did, the energy would be all wrong. Someone who lets shyness get in the way of their happiness will most likely never ask for what they want. Such a person is ruled by a fear of failure, so you don't need to invite them into your life.

Over fifteen years ago, while working in my one and only office job, I pestered my friends with this very question. This guy had a girlfriend, whom he cheated on more than once. He wasn't truly interested in me, but he was shy and used women's interest in him to bolster his self-esteem. He drank too much, and he didn't have an interesting personality to back up that pensive exterior. Life passed him by while he remained in a job he hated and hung around with people whose company he did not truly enjoy. Had I listened to my instincts, I would have known all of this at the time.

Everything we do as a couple is scheduled around my boyfriend's timeline. We will move in together when he turns thirty, we'll get married when he feels ready, and so on. Should I be fine with this arrangement?

Absolutely not. This relationship is weighted in his favour. The balance of power should naturally shift between the two of you at different times and in different scenarios. Any relationship dynamic where one partner always dominates the other is simply unhealthy. This relationship is not nearly good enough for you. Continue to work on yourself, engage in therapy, and meditate regularly. As you begin to see your true worth, your need for a balanced and mutually respectful relationship will outweigh any residual need to hold onto this unbalanced one. Your boyfriend may respond to your emergent strength with renewed respect and start to treat you as an equal. If he is not a decent guy deep down, he will fear it. Being a strong woman, you will not stand for this; you'll break up with him and move on to better things and a better relationship.

My family disapproves of my new partner. He is of a different social class and he didn't go to college. They believe he is after my money. I'm not that well off; I'm a middle-income civil servant. Should I listen to them?

Your family's opinion is distressing you for a reason. While you may be angered and disgusted by their snobbery and prejudice, as long as you hold on to that anger, you are letting them control you. You are allowing yourself to be consumed by it. Make the decision on your own terms and for the sake of your relationship, thereby releasing your need for their approval. Allow them their right to think what they will of you, your partner and your relationship. The view is always different depending on where you're standing. Their life experience is different from yours, so they see things differently. Try to accept that they are not consciously trying to sabotage your love life; they simply dislike your partner and choose not to change their perspective.

On the other hand, is it possible that you're riled by their disapproval because you are having misgivings about your partner? A therapist once said to me that a man's poor taste in shoes is not a problem if you already like him, but if you haven't yet started to fall for him, those shoes could be a big problem indeed. They may provide the excuse you're seeking to dismiss him. If you truly adore your partner, other people's opinions won't matter to you.

My new boyfriend talks to me about how beautiful other women are, as if I am a male friend of his. This makes me feel invisible and unattractive. He goes to great lengths to reassure me that he does not think beauty is that important. Advice?

You are not his male friend; you are his lovely girlfriend and he needs to start treating you as such. How dare he reassure you that he will not be tempted by the beauty of other women and that he will remain faithful to you—his dowdy, unattractive mate? If he is constantly noticing other women's looks, then looks are important to him. Perhaps he doesn't find you attractive and he's trying to convince himself that physical attraction is not necessary for a loving relationship. On the other hand, he may be terribly insecure and attempting to damage your self-esteem in order to make himself feel better. Either way, you need to cut him loose. Unless he apologises, tells you he thinks you're the most beautiful woman he's ever laid eyes on, and spends the rest of his days proving it, don't give him another minute of your time. Let him walk. He can spend the rest of his life ogling other women to his heart's desire. You deserve to have someone who appreciates your beauty and gives you his undivided attention.

I am still pining over a lost love. He has recently gotten married and I feel as if I will never be able to move on or find love again. Any advice?

You will move on when you meet someone you like more. At this moment in time, you may feel as if there is no one in this world who could measure up to this past love of yours, but just wait until you notice that really handsome man on your morning train or a friend brings her charming co-worker to your New Year's Eve party. The nicest falling-in-love experiences are the discoveries, the unexpected revelations, when that nice, friendly guy suddenly looks like a potential life partner. It's the loveliest surprise of all. You will move on the moment you meet someone more special to you than your previous love. It will happen. A good friend recently said to me, on the subject of her moving past heartbreak to find a new man, the heart can be very fickle when it comes to love, and sometimes that's a good thing!

I have a few highlights in my hair and it seems to me that men love blondes. Should I go the whole hog and bleach my entire head? I'm not popular with men at the moment. Your thoughts?

Only go blonde if you want to; don't do it for the sole purpose of making yourself more attractive to men. If you're not feeling good about yourself and you change your hair colour or any other aspect of your appearance just to make yourself more appealing to the opposite sex, you will not feel any more confident than you did before. In the words of Shakespeare, "To thine own self be true." When you love your look and you feel that it truly reflects your personality, style and attitude, you will shine. You are infinitely more likely to make an authentic love connection when you are being your true self.

Should we have discussed marriage early in our relationship? We've been dating for almost a year and I want to appear chilled out, but I would really like to know sooner rather than later if he intends to propose.

Trust your instincts. You will know if your relationship is moving towards marriage from the general conversations you have had over the past year. If this man is a closed book and he never shows his feelings, then maybe he is not the right man for you. It is essential for your emotional well-being that you have a partner who supports you by communicating with and caring for you; he cannot do that if he is distant and removed. No matter how smart, funny or handsome he is, unless he is affectionate, tender, understanding and kind, he is not someone with whom you should be planning a future. You deserve a kind, loving man. He doesn't have to wear his heart on his sleeve, but if he is incapable of opening up and showing love then he will never be able to nurture or satisfy you in the way that a romantic partner should.

Romantic relationships at work are frowned upon. Is this the reason my boss hasn't asked me out?

You may have overestimated his interest in you. Perhaps he likes you but not enough to risk his reputation at work. Either way, why are you losing sleep over whether this relationship is meant to be? If he really liked you, he'd find a way to be with you. Forget about him for now. You want a man who will move mountains to be with you. Take his failure to ask you out as a lack of initiative on his part. Let him figure out what he needs to do. Do not plot and plan to accidentally bump into him in the corridor or go for lunch at the same time he does every day. Such behaviour is beneath you and it is very unattractive. Be nice to yourself. Love and respect yourself, and others will mirror this back to you.

Should I tell the guy I've just met about my child?

If he likes you, he won't mind. Tell him the same way you'd tell a friend that you're still getting to know. Don't drop a bombshell and run for shelter. When the topic of children arises naturally, you can mention it and tell him about your situation. If he doesn't want to get involved with you after learning that you have a child, it's clearly not going to work out between the two of you. He can look for love elsewhere, as can you.

I'm obsessed with a man I see almost every day in the gym. It has been two years now since I suggested we play squash together. He has not taken me up on my offer. What is my next move?

Your next move is to move on. You should value yourself too much to tolerate the indignity of stalking someone. Have some pride. Even if you think he's the most wonderful man you have ever laid eyes on, he does not return your affections. You deserve to be loved and appreciated. Clear out this baggage and make room for the wonderful man who is making his way into your life.

I have small breasts. Is this the reason I'm still single?

In my twenties, I had never given much thought to the size of my breasts. As girls, we learn from our mothers how to feel about our own bodies. Since my mother never expressed any dissatisfaction with her petite frame, I accepted my breasts as just another part of me. But when I lost weight in my late twenties, my breasts became a lot smaller. The more I focussed my attention on this part of my body, the more deeply unhappy I became with it. When I asked a newly acquired friend, who was very proud of her own larger-than-average chest, if my breast size might explain men's lack of interest in me, she replied, "I'm not saying that's the reason, but it is definitely a possibility."

Looking back, I can see that it was not my bra size, my red hair, my freckles or any of my other physical traits that were keeping me single. I understand that I had a complete lack of faith in myself. Instead of investigating this issue further in therapy, I pinned my difficulties in finding love on a physical trait, one that I sought to modify. At twenty-eight, I saw breast augmentation as the answer to all my relationship problems but didn't have the cash to fund this whim. Now, I'm glad I didn't undergo surgery, as my body was not the problem.

There are many factors at play in physical attraction, and different people find all kinds of different things sexy and beautiful. A man who is truly attracted to you is attracted to *you*, and not to a single body part or its shape or size. Love your body and be proud of it. Being happy and comfortable in your own skin is the best way to supercharge your magnetism.

The Knowledge

When someone holds a strong, unshakable belief about themselves, they will ultimately make that belief a reality. When you know in your heart that you're fully capable of attaining whatever you want, you can relax and let destiny unfold. Your future has already taken hold in your mind as something positive and interesting. You take it for granted that you will someday manifest the loving relationship that you deserve. It's like dreaming of Christmas in September—you know it will roll around sooner than you think. Moaning about how it's not here yet will only frustrate you and others. Remember, the lead up to a highly anticipated pleasure is often underrated. Savour it, instead of wishing it away.

If you make up your mind that you will meet a wonderful man at the right time, it shall be so. **Know that it can happen just like that—and it will.**

"This book arrives just in time in a jaded, post-dating app world of unfulfill-ing 'situation-ships'. Drawing both from her own hard-earned life lessons and a diverse range of philosophies Penelope has crafted a game-changing step-by-step guide designed to 'hack' the world of dating. Not afraid to share and be vulner-able, detailing her own highs and lows, Penelope coaches the reader in search of a meaningful relationship. For anyone agonizing over whether to end a 'blah' courtship (hint end it now) or wondering why he didn't text back, this book is a no-nonsense manifesto packed with actionable steps that will save so much time and heartache."

Dr Sidhbh Gallagher, Irish double-boarded plastic surgeon practicing in the USA, the focus of her career is gender affirmation surgery.

"I've often been advised by my elders, friends and Instagram captions that I should learn to really 'love myself'. While I can attest to falling in and out of love with many people and things, at 25, the concept of self-love has proved intimidat-ing and hard. Until now, I had hoped this might just develop with experience and maturity but Penelope's advice and anecdotes, which are in equal parts comfort-ing and enlightening, have inspired me to take the bull by the horns, open my heart and see where it might take me."

Doireann Ní Ghlacáin, TV Presenter with TG4.

"Ever started running out of faith that your perfect partner is really is out there? This practical self-help guide written from the heart by Penelope Winters is an absolute must read. The book brings you on a journey which many of us will recognise with plenty of laughs along the way. It delves into the ups and downs of the dating world reminding us to always be the best version of ourselves, rather than a poor imitation of somebody else. You won't be able to put it down."

Laura Wood, www.laurawood.ie, breakfast show presenter, East Coast FM.

"A humorous and inspiring guide to dating and looking for real love in 2020. Read with an open heart and mind, you will learn something that will lead you closer to the love of your life. I also fell in love with Gilbert Blythe reading Anne of Green Gables growing up, Penelope's book is a great reminder that there are Gilberts out there dying to meet an Anne Shirley."

Nadine Reid, 'Woman of the Year—Entertainment' Irish Tatler Awards 2019, Guest TV Presenter Virgin Media, MC & Makeup Artist.

"If you are looking for a partner who shares your core values and goals, who loves and respects you and whose eyes light up when you walk into the room then this would be one of the best books to read. An absolutely great book!"

Oksana Lobanova, actress and artist.

"This is very relatable and liberating. It has restored my faith in finding love. I will be turning this into my second bible and will be sharing it with a lot of my friends. We are all deserving of real love!"

Mona Lxsa, DJ and founder of Gxrl Code.

"A modern single woman's bible to surviving, and remaining confident, in the tumultuous present day dating world."

Emma Nolan, a twenty six year old broadcaster with Dublin's FM104 with a strong passion for music.

"Here is an opportunity to renew your hope and excitement about finding love! I really appreciate how Winters brings our focus back to the self in this book and helps us to understand that through care, love and respect for ourselves we can become our own advocate and transform our approach to meeting potential partners. We are reminded and inspired to trust, and everything will unfold from there. I'm currently re-entering the dating scene and grateful to pick up some refreshing views and encouragement about the mad world of meeting romantic prospects."

Alice Marr, waitress on RTE's First Dates Ireland and Yoga Teacher.

"Honest and refreshing. It's so much more positive to encourage women to embrace who they are and love themselves—thank you Penelope!"

Lauren Kelly, broadcaster & new mum.

"A dating manifesto! Powerful, direct and truly helpful to women who are looking for the love of their lives. Penelope is really out to help women return to themselves, and find their true love. Enjoy, and do yourselves a favour, try Penelope's techniques, and above all, love yourself! Believe in your ability to find love. This book will NO DOUBT help you on this journey."

Ethan Miles, First Dates Ireland bartender.

"Honest, insightful and life-affirming."

*Goggle Box Ireland's the **Cabra Girls**.*

Printed in Great Britain
by Amazon

42574067R00099